W9-BNW-587

The
Ultimate
BARBECUE
SAUCE
Cookbook

Jim Auchmutey
Susan Puckett

LONGSTREET PRESS, INC.
Atlanta, Georgia

For Pam and Jim

Published by
LONGSTREET PRESS, INC.
A subsidiary of Cox Newspapers,
A division of Cox Enterprises, Inc.
2140 Newmarket Parkway
Suite 118, Marietta, GA 30067

Copyright © 1995 by Jim Auchmutey and Susan Puckett

All rights reserved. No part of this book may be reproduced in any
form or by any means without the prior written permission of the
Publisher, excepting brief quotations used in connection with
reviews, written specifically for inclusion in a magazine or
newspaper.

Printed in the United States of America

1st printing 1995

Library of Congress Catalog Card Number: 94-74236

ISBN 1-56352-201-2

This book was printed by Quebecor/Kingsport, Kingsport, Tennessee.
Electronic film prep and separations by Advertising Technologies Inc., Atlanta, GA

Book design by Audrey Graham
Jacket design by Jill Dible
Photograph by Al Clayton

Many thanks to FUJI

CONTENTS

Getting Sauced . . . *3*

Great American Barbecue Sauces . . . *19*

Fooling with Fruit . . . *41*

Anything Goes . . . *63*

International Flavors . . . *85*

Different Treats for Different Meats . . . *111*

Dry Rubs . . . *129*

By the Bottle . . . *143*

Acknowledgments . . . *152*

Index . . . *153*

The Ultimate

BARBECUE

SAUCE

Cookbook

Getting Sauced

Hot and sweet and red and greasy,
I could eat a gallon easy:
Barbecue sauce!
Lay it on, hoss.

— Roy Blount Jr.
"Ode to Barbecue Sauce"

*B*arbecue people — the hard-core, hardwood types, anyway — like to say that barbecue sauce isn't very important. That it's the meat that matters, or the fire or the fuel or the smoke, anything but the sauce. One Georgia pit man put it this way: "It's like a woman and hair. She's better with it, but it don't make her a woman." (This poet's name is William "Cockroach" Tingle, but that's another story...)

Well, sauce probably *doesn't* matter as much as the meat and some of those other things. But if it's not important, why are barbecue people so peculiar about the marinades, mops, sops and rubs they use? If the secret isn't in the sauce, how come so many sauces are secret?

Maurice Bessinger of Columbia, S.C., says he ducks behind a black curtain like some kind of a pit witch when he mixes up his special mustard sauce — a recipe he has entrusted to only two other people, both blood relations.

Spring Creek Bar-B-Que in Arlington, Texas, filed suit against a former employee, accusing him of pilfering its sauce recipe to use at a competing restaurant. Sticky-fingered attorneys got big bucks to prove that Sauce Exhibit A constituted an infringement of Sauce Exhibit B.

John "Big Daddy" Bishop of Tuscaloosa, Ala., mumbles something about "this 'n' that" when people ask him what's in his rib sauce, which they do every day the sun comes up. Press him, and he'll tell how the Pit Boss in the Sky came to him in a dream that was so vivid it included ingredients.

It's not important?

Why, then, are there so many vanity sauces — barbecue people putting out their own label, scores and scores of them, with names like Crazy Jim's and Swine Wine and Dragon's Breath, all convinced that if the world would only taste their sauce, it'd throw away all those grocery store brands?

Whatever they say, barbecue purists know that barbecue sauce matters a lot. It's more than a condiment that tastes so good you want to suck your fingernails. It's the essence of things that make our juices flow. It's about family, tradition, individuality, pride in place, old stories told over new fires. It's about life and the eternal quest for the perfect balance between ting and tang.

"This identity people have with certain barbecue styles is rather profound," says Charles Kovacik, a geography professor at the University of South Carolina who has studied and mapped the state's sauce regions. He's seen it a dozen times: Someone strays into an alien barbecue joint, orders a plate of pig meat, sniffs at the unfamiliar sauce and exclaims, "This ain't barbecue!"

The Carolinas, of course, are the Balkans of barbecue. The

mustard people around Columbia look down their noses at the tomato people in North Carolina, and they all seem vaguely heathen to the vinegar folks east of Raleigh (one of whom opened a barbecue stand in Maryland with a sign that warned, "We don't hold with tomatoes").

That sauce, Carolina spiced vinegar, was probably America's original barbecue dressing. Colonists learned early on how to barbecue hogs from slaves and Native Americans. To enhance flavor and mask bad meat, they used a clear, vinegar sauce derived from the tomato-less English ketchup of the day.

No one knows exactly when the first tomato barbecue sauce came along, but it well could have happened before 1824. In her cookbook published that year, *The Virginia Housewife*, Mary Randolph included a tomato sauce recipe that would serve nicely as a base for the finish they use at your local rib shack. Tomato-based barbecue sauces are still by far the most popular style.

Barbecue sauce remained a regional phenomenon of the South and Midwest into the 1900s. Not until after World War II, when backyard grilling became part of the suburban good life, did bottled sauces become widely available at stores. The first national brand, Kraft, appeared in the 1950s.

Today, Americans spend $480 million a year on barbecue sauce, making it the third-largest-selling condiment after salsa and ketchup. Six national companies account for four-fifths of sales, according to Packaged Facts, a New York market research firm. The remainder is split between a growing number of regional and local labels, many of them in the South where, for reasons of culture and climate, use is the heaviest.

That's where we come in. We're both native Southerners — Susan from Mississippi, Jim from Georgia — and have had sauce on our lips since we first learned to stretch out a vowel. We've tasted many styles of barbecue over the years and have come to appreciate the smoke-cooking of Jamaica, Japan and a dozen other cultures — even South Carolina's.

In researching and writing this book, we've learned a lot, and we've learned from the masters. We've pulled together the tastiest ideas from cook-off teams and international cuisines, from famous old barbecue joints and acclaimed new restaurants with cutting-edge chefs, and we've tested every shirt-splattering one of them. We've also (in our final chapter) collected the most interesting bottled sauces from around the nation and chosen 50 of the best.

We found that sauce is an easy way to get in on the fun of barbecue. Pass a bowl of homemade at your next cookout, and you'll get more compliments than a year's worth of barbecues with the store-bought stuff. You don't have to dig a pit. You don't have to shovel coals. You just need a saucepan, some measuring utensils and a few common ingredients.

Those and a little imagination.

Saucemaking 101

It's hard to screw up barbecue sauce. It won't turn lumpy or break its silky emulsion like a delicate béchamel or hollandaise. Unlike baking a cake, it won't fall because you overbeat the eggs. About the worst things that can happen are that it might be too tart, too sweet, too thick, too thin, too bland, too salty — all of which can be fixed by adding a little of this or that.

The art of creating a great barbecue sauce has less to do with technique than taste buds. Some of the most finely tuned taste buds in barbecue belong to Chef Paul Kirk of Kansas City. Since entering his first cook-off in 1981, he has won such a reputation for saucemaking that companies hire him to "break" famous blends like Arthur Bryant's.

At the barbecue classes Kirk teaches around the country, he usually starts students on ketchup-based sauces because they're so easy to make. To get them in the spirit, Kirk tells students about an Ethiopian who took one of his courses with the aim of Americanizing his native cuisine. "He made a dry rub with *20 ingredients* in it," Kirk says. "I was pretty dubious; that seemed excessive. I was shocked when his ribs turned out to be the best in the class."

Hence Kirk's First Law of Saucemaking: Experiment; you never know until you try.

Other rules:

- There are no rules. They say rosemary goes with lamb or beef, but it's great on chicken and pork, too. You wouldn't know that unless you broke rules.
- Work with small quantities so you don't waste a lot of ingredients on the inevitable failures.
- Don't overdo a favorite ingredient. People always think if a little

of something tastes good, a lot will taste better. Big mistake.
- Think balance. Play sweet against sour, hot against mild.
- Don't clutter the sauce with stuff that doesn't count. When Kirk sees a recipe with an endless list of trace ingredients, he figures most of them add little or nothing to the finished sauce.

THE BUILDING BLOCKS

A sauce is only as good as its parts. Most barbecue sauces are a blend of tart, sweet, salty, spicy, tomatoey flavors. Tomato is usually the dominant note, but even that rule has many exceptions. Some sauces are vinegar-based; others use mustard as the lead ingredient; still others are carried by molasses or another sweetener.

Here are the major flavors and how to achieve them:

Tomatoey: Ketchup, tomato paste, tomato purée, tomato sauce, canned tomatoes, chili sauce, even — argh! — tomato soup have all been bases for barbecue sauce.

Tart: Vinegar usually provides the twangy accent, although lemon or lime juice also does the trick. Some sauces contain multiple tart elements. Distilled vinegar is the most sour, followed closely by cider vinegar, which also adds an appley note. Wine and herb vinegars take the flavor into slightly different directions. Wine or beer lends a more subtle tanginess, although they're generally used with a more acidic ingredient. Mustard also adds pucker.

Sweet: White or brown sugar are the most obvious choices, but you've got plenty of others — molasses, corn syrup, honey, maple syrup, fruit juice, jams, jellies. A shot of Coca-Cola, bourbon, rum or liqueur also sugars sauce.

Salty: You don't want to overdo it, but it's hard to make a balanced sauce without some salt. It doesn't all have to come from the shaker, though; soy sauce, Worcestershire, steak sauce, liquid smoke and various seasoning blends can achieve the same effect — and add a layer of flavor.

Spicy: Most saucemakers would agree that ground pepper — black, red, white or a combination — is essential. Chili peppers have been turning up lately as well. Mustard can add spiciness. Garlic and onion, in fresh or powdered form, are usually present. Beyond that, your options are limited only by the contents of your spice rack.

Rich: You can make a perfectly good sauce without a drop of fat. On the other hand, there are some sauces with a rich, creamy quality that only butter, oil or some other fatty substance can provide. Sometimes butter is used at the beginning of cooking to sauté vegetable ingredients; other times it's melted in toward the end. Some fats contribute as much flavor as they do richness — among them, the sinful secret ingredient at Sonny Bryan's Smokehouse in Dallas: beef drippings.

About those terms

In this book, we've stretched the definition of barbecue sauce to include a variety of things people put on grilled or smoked meat. What we haven't included are cold salsas and relishes, simply because there are already a number of cookbooks devoted exclusively to them.

Here are some terms you'll run across and how we use them:

Rub: A combination of seasonings — dry or paste — rubbed into meat before (and sometimes during) cooking.

Mop or sop: A thin liquid used to baste meat during cooking, sometimes applied with a mop. Mops and sops can be as simple as vinegar or beer.

Marinade: A liquid used for soaking meat to flavor and perhaps tenderize it. Marinades usually contain vinegar, fruit or vegetable juices, oil and seasonings. To tenderize, it must contain an acidic ingredient such as lemon or lime juice, wine, vinegar or yogurt.

Finishing sauce: A sauce applied during the last 15 to 30 minutes of cooking to form a glaze. Usually contains tomatoes and sugar, which, if applied earlier, would burn.

Table sauce: All-purpose term for any sauce tasty enough to be served with the finished dish.

Dip: A thinner table sauce into which barbecue can be dipped.

Storage and Safety

Containers: Since most sauces and marinades contain acidic ingredients that may react with certain metals, it's best to store them in glass or plastic containers.

How long will it keep? Some sauces, including many that are simply vinegar and a few spices, will keep indefinitely and do not need to be refrigerated. Most tomato-based barbecue sauces will retain their quality in the refrigerator for at least two weeks. After that, some of the spices could grow stronger or turn bitter. For longer storage, divide the sauce up into smaller containers and freeze.

If the sauce contains broth or some other meat product, don't keep it longer than a few days in the refrigerator. After that, freeze it.

Safe marinating: If you're planning to baste with the same marinade the raw meat's been soaking in, heat it first to kill the bacteria. Same applies if you're planning to use it as a table sauce. As soon as the meat goes on the grill, stick the marinade container in the sink and get a clean one — unless you want to risk food poisoning.

First the Fire

To our minds, barbecue means meat cooked slowly by the smoke of a fire that's mostly coals. Grilling is quite another thing, calling for fast cooking over a hotter fire. We realize that most Americans don't draw this distinction as religiously as Southerners; many of you use barbecue to mean any sort of cook-out. OK, we'll be ecumenical about this. There's no reason not to be since most of the sauces in this book work well with both types of smoke-cooking — and with smokeless cooking, for that matter.

There are almost as many barbecue contraptions out there as people in funny-looking aprons to use them. On the inexpensive end, there's your garden-variety backyard charcoal or gas grill, which everyone who wears pants has used. On the other end, there's the multichamber cooker — fire in one chamber, meat and smoke in another — which can get as elaborate as those $30,000 land yachts some cook-off teams haul from fairground to fairground.

In between is the humble water smoker — probably the most reasonable way to get smoked flavor onto your table without digging a pit where the pansies are. Like a booster rocket, the water smoker has three stages: The bottom holds a basin for coals; the middle holds a bowl for steam-making water; the top holds one or two racks for meat. Four hours in one of these babies and your baby-back ribs are crying to be cuddled.

Cookers generally come in gas, electric and charcoal models. Most Americans use charcoal, followed by gas. With gas or electric, you just turn them on. Charcoal cookers take a little more effort.

There are several ways to build a charcoal fire — an electric coal starter is probably the easiest — but most people do it the way it says to on the back of the charcoal bag. Build a pyramid of coals, douse it with lighter fluid, let it soak in, then light. It'll probably take half an hour before the chemicals burn off and the coals take on that orange-gray glow that says, "Bring it on!"

Grilled foods such as steak or swordfish cook well over direct heat, meaning they're directly over the coals. Slower-cooking foods like ribs and beef brisket do better over indirect heat, meaning they're over a drip pan set in the coals to discourage fat flare-ups.

However you cook, the key to good flavor is smoke. Professional barbecuers get that flavor by laying a hardwood fire. Recreational barbecuers can get it by using hardwood chips soaked in water at least 30 minutes so they smolder when thrown on the heat. Different woods have different tastes. Apple and other fruitwoods lend a slight sweetness. Mesquite and oak give an earthy flavor. Hickory, the most commonly used, has the strong flavor most people associate with barbecue.

Playing with fire

Cooking times and methods for different types of meat vary widely depending on how hot your fire is and the type of equipment you're using. There are many books that cover barbecuing and grilling techniques, so we'll leave the details to them. (You'll find some of the best ones listed at the end of the book.) In the meantime, here are some basic cooking instructions for the three cuts of meat most identified with American barbecue: ribs, pork shoulders and briskets. Many of the sauces in this book go with other smoked dishes as well, but we imagine you've figured out how to grill chicken or fish or hamburgers. These fellows take more doing.

PORK RIBS

The basic types used for barbecuing are:

Spareribs: Mostly bone and little meat, it's America's favorite rib; an elongated slab cut from just behind the pork shoulder.

Loin or baby-back ribs: Shorter than spareribs; generally meatier and more expensive.

Country-style ribs: The shoulder end of a bone-in loin. Be careful not to overcook; their meat is leaner than other ribs and therefore has a greater tendency to dry out and toughen.

Trim excess fat from ribs if desired; some people like to parboil them for at least 3 to 4 minutes, or up to 15 to 20 minutes, when the meat starts to shrink from the end of the bone. This helps get rid of excess fat as well as tenderize the ribs.

Season with a dry rub, or marinate if desired.

On the grill: In a covered grill, arrange medium-hot coals around a drip pan. Center meat over drip pan, lower hood and grill for about 1 hour. Baste every 10 minutes or so.

After ribs have been grilling about 1 hour, brush with a finishing sauce. Grill about 15 or 30 minutes longer, basting occasionally with the sauce, until ribs are nicely browned and juices run clear when meat is cut into.

In the smoker: After sprinkling with rub, place ribs bone side down on top rack, close dome and leave the thing alone. Keep middle tray filled with water. Keep fire stoked so temperature gauge remains in the low ideal range, a little over 200 degrees. Brush with finishing sauce after 3 1/2 hours. Ribs should be ready after 4 hours.

In the oven: Place ribs, bone side down, in a single layer in a shallow roasting pan. Apply rub, if using. Bake in a 350-degree oven for 1 hour; drain off fat. Cover ribs with barbecue sauce; bake 30 to 60 minutes longer or until well-done.

PORK SHOULDER

This is the stuff served on buns or white bread that many Southerners associate with real barbecue. It's a great way to showcase any kind of barbecue sauce, tomato or vinegar-based, and it freezes well.

Trim fat from 5- to 6-pound pork shoulder or butt.

If desired, cover with dry rub or marinade; if using marinade, cover and refrigerate overnight.

In the smoker: Bring meat to room temperature and cook in a water smoker over medium heat about 6 hours or until meat thermometer reaches 160 degrees. Baste with sauce during last hour, if desired.

In the oven: Preheat to 350 degrees. Roast, covered, for 2 hours; uncover and roast 1 hour longer, basting with sauce occasionally.

To serve: Slice, shred or pull and chop the meat. Serve soaked in sauce or with sauce on side. Pile onto buns and top with coleslaw, if desired.

BEEF BRISKET

The national barbecue of Texas comes from the cow's breast. They love it in Kansas City, too.

In the smoker: After sprinkling with rub, place brisket fat side up and close dome. Maintain fire to keep temperature gauge around 200. After 3 1/2 hours, wrap brisket loosely in heavy-duty foil. Sprinkle more rub, drizzle with beer (if desired) and tent foil over brisket. Close dome and continue smoking another 3 1/2 hours.

On the grill: Rub brisket with beer, sprinkle with dry rub and refrigerate 1 hour. Preheat gas grill on medium setting or ignite charcoal and burn until ashen. Place 2 cups of soaked wood chips in foil pan and put on top of coals.

Center meat over foil pan to catch juices. Close grill lid; smoke for 30 minutes. Add 2 cups more wood chips; turn meat. Smoke 30 minutes longer. Transfer meat to large square of heavy foil; sprinkle each side with 2 tablespoons of rub. Pour 1 cup of the beer over meat; close foil tightly.

At this point, it can be finished in preheated 350-degree oven for 2 hours or returned to grill and cooked 2 hours. (Check meat after 1 hour. If it is dry, add 1 cup of water and reseal foil tightly.)

To serve: Slice thinly. Don't worry if the meat looks pink and uncooked near the surface. That's a smoke ring, and it comes from good smoke penetration. Think of it as your door prize for a job well done.

The joys of judging

There are hundreds of barbecue cook-offs in this great carnivorous country. Most of them include sauce contests. Jim judged at one of the largest, his own state's championship, the Big Pig Jig in Vienna, Ga. It was his first barbecue sauce contest.

Judging, I had been told, was a solemn undertaking. Some educated palates have adjudicated dozens of taste-offs. Some actually take classes to learn how to sharpen their senses. I, on the other hand, had exactly one qualification: a working mouth.

It was Friday night in South Georgia, and the fairgrounds along I-75 were beginning to haze over with the smoke of hogs hitting the hickory. While I was waiting for the judging to begin, I noticed a paragraph in the rules allowing only "non-poisonous substances and sauces." Can't be too careful.

The other judges and I were sequestered in a tent, penned in by a chain-link fence to keep us away from 130 cook-off teams. Each crew's sauce was assigned a number and delivered to us in foam cups. Six samples made their way to my table, where six of us waited with pencils, score sheets and loaves of white bread.

What, no meat?

I was informed that this contest was part of the Memphis in May circuit, and that their rules called for "naked judging." (The other big league barbecue circuit, sponsored by the Kansas City Barbecue Society, judges sauces with unseasoned meat — fully clothed, I take it.)

Whatever the reasons, it struck me as a terrible waste to have all this fine sauce without something to splash it on. I couldn't help thinking about it as we sat there spooning and dipping one cup of red after another, our eyes rolled back in concentration as we weighed tangy questions of jurisprudence.

Finally I blurted it out: "Kind of like prison rations, isn't it?"

A veteran judge glared at me from across the table. "Just be glad this isn't a wild game cook-off," he said. "They expect you to eat *all* that stuff."

GREAT AMERICAN BARBECUE SAUCES

*Y*ou've got to feel good about a country that can create this much flavor. Talk about a melting pot. Carolina tart, Texas heat, Kansas City sweet — when you think of all the things people have concocted to slosh on barbecue, it's enough to make you stand up and pledge allegiance.

In barbecue, as in other matters, Americans are notoriously opposed to central planning. We do, however, reserve states' rights to sauce as we please. The Carolinas, with their breakaway republics of vinegar and mustard, reserve this right in spades.

The rest of the country is less extreme, with many sauces that are more or less the same no matter where you happen to be. But there are discernible patterns. As a rule, the Deep South prefers a tomato-and-vinegar sauce that gets thicker the farther west you go. Texans, if they use sauce at all, tend to go for sweet red stuff. Kansas Citians have a taste for molasses and chili powder. Northerners like smoke flavoring. Southwesterners like it hot. Westerners play around with wine and fruit blends.

Think of the next few pages, then, as a heritage trip for your taste buds, a full-color road map to American barbeculture, a guided tour through a stove-top Smithsonian.

This sauce is your sauce, this sauce is my sauce . . .

This is probably what comes to mind when most Americans think of barbecue sauce. Thick, sweet and as deep-red as crushed velvet, Kaycee has become the most popular regional sauce in America. Two variations — K.C. Masterpiece (created by Kansas City psychiatrist Rich Davis) and Bull's-Eye — account for a quarter of the nation's sauce market.

Kansas City is a crossroads of barbecue styles, the place where Southern ribmeisters, Southwestern beef-eaters and Midwestern meat-cutters mingled to create something like Barbecue Heaven. The sauces are just as varied, the most famous being the grainy, rust-colored stuff at Arthur Bryant's, which Calvin Trillin proclaimed the best restaurant in the world. Calvin was clearly sauce-drunk when he wrote that, but then most Kansas Citians are. Let's put it this way: Kansas City is the only place we've ever been passed on the street by a barbecue sauce truck.

Paul Kirk, one of the cook-off circuit's best cooks, gave us this recipe. We can see why he bills himself as "the Kansas City Baron of Barbecue."

Makes about 4 1/2 cups

3/4 cup packed brown sugar
1 to 2 tablespoons ground black pepper
1 1 1/4-ounce package chili seasoning
2 teaspoons dry mustard
1 teaspoon powdered ginger
1/2 teaspoon ground allspice
1/4 teaspoon ground red pepper
1/4 teaspoon ground mace
1 cup distilled vinegar
1/4 cup molasses
1/4 cup water
1 32-ounce bottle ketchup
1 to 3 teaspoons liquid smoke (optional)

- In a large saucepan, combine brown sugar, black pepper, chili seasoning, mustard, ginger, allspice, red pepper and mace.
- Add vinegar, molasses and water. Stir until dry ingredients are dissolved.
- Stir in ketchup. Add liquid smoke if desired. Bring to a boil, stirring constantly to avoid spattering.
- Reduce heat to low, and simmer, covered, for 30 minutes. Serve warm.
- Refrigerate unused sauce up to several weeks.

Uses: As a finishing and table sauce for beef, pork and chicken. Also good in meatloaf.

Dr. Barbecue's Carolina Mustard Sauce

Makes about 1 3/4 cups

3/4 cup yellow mustard
3/4 cup red wine vinegar
1/4 cup sugar
1 1/2 tablespoons butter or margarine
2 teaspoons salt
1/2 tablespoon Worcestershire sauce
1 1/4 teaspoons ground black pepper
1/2 teaspoon Tabasco sauce

- In a medium saucepan, combine ingredients, stirring to blend.
- Over low heat, simmer 30 minutes. Let stand at room temperature 1 hour before using.
- Refrigerate unused sauce up to several weeks.

Uses: As a baste or table sauce with pork or chicken. Slap it on hot dogs, too.

Another Ph.B.: South Carolina's Charles Kovacik isn't the only academic to research barbecue. At Western Kentucky University, John Marshall wrote his master's thesis on "Barbecue in Western Kentucky: An Ethnographic Study."

Charles Kovacik may be the world's first barbecue cartographer. When the Michigan native moved south a few years back, he was amazed by how strongly people in different parts of the Carolinas identify with different sauces. Charles is a geography professor at the University of South Carolina, so naturally he launched an academic inquiry. He and colleague John Winberry ate at more than a hundred barbecue joints and devised a map of South Carolina sauce regions that makes the state look like the former Yugoslavia. In the process, Dr. K shed some of his professional objectivity. At a 1994 academic conference in North Carolina, he delivered a paper called "South Carolina: Epicenter of Southern Barbecue." "I get a lot of North Carolina hecklers," he says.

The tribal sauce around Columbia has a mustard base. The professor got this recipe from his church, where they cook whole hogs at fund-raisers. "I suppose the sauce will work on less than a whole hog," he says, "but it just isn't right!"

GOD'S OWN DREAM SAUCE

Few barbecue sauces have a cult following as large as Dreamland's. The sauce from this little rib shack near the University of Alabama induces ecstasy among players, coaches and sportswriters nationwide. The matching blazers on TV practically salivate about it. We had to go to Tuscaloosa to investigate — and eat.

Dreamland isn't much to look at: just a small house with a gravel lot on Jug Factory Road. Inside, the dark room is lined with photos of fans like Don Shula, Bobby Bowden and Hank Williams Jr. Everyone loves the ribs, but it's the sauce — a little sweet, a little hot — that really seduces them. Cold sufferers have been known to come in and turn up a jar to clear their sinuses. Students have smuggled samples into the agriculture lab at the university and tried (unsuccessfully) to replicate it.

Last year a writer for *Men's Journal* came up with a recipe that Jeannette Bishop-Hall, Dreamland's manager, says comes pretty close. We tried it.

Makes about 2 quarts

1 28-ounce can tomato purée
1/3 cup yellow mustard
3 cups water
1 1/2 cups cider vinegar
1/4 cup dark corn syrup
2 tablespoons lemon juice
2 tablespoons sugar
2 tablespoons packed brown sugar
2 tablespoons chili powder
1 tablespoon dry mustard
1 tablespoon paprika
2 teaspoons ground red pepper
2 teaspoons onion powder
1 teaspoon salt
1 teaspoon ground black pepper
1/2 teaspoon garlic powder

- In a large saucepan, whisk together the tomato purée and mustard until smooth. Stir in remaining ingredients.
- Bring to a boil. Reduce heat to low, and simmer for 30 minutes, stirring occasionally. Serve warm.
- Refrigerate unused sauce up to several weeks.

Uses: As a finishing and table sauce for pork ribs and just about anything else you can put in your mouth. To order Dreamland sauce, see final chapter.

Let there be barbecue: In Daniel 7:5 the Old Testament prophet relates a prophetic dream: "And behold another beast, a second, like to a bear, and it raised up itself on one side, and it had three ribs in the mouth of it between the teeth of it, and they said thus unto it, Arise, devour much flesh."

Too bland. "Well, you know, I've got an ulcer and can't eat anything too spicy," she confessed. "I usually eat Heinz."

So we showed the recipe to her father, John "Big Daddy" Bishop Sr., a great big slab of a man who created the sauce with his wife when they opened Dreamland in 1958. "Shoot," he said, dripping disgust, "that's a mile off. Ain't none of my stuff in there."

What stuff?

"Dog if I can tell you. God came to me in a dream and gave me this sauce. You see, it's kind of hard for me to talk about."

We hope this isn't sacrilegious, Big Daddy, but we figured it would be in the Dreamland tradition to give it the good old college try. Here goes.

B.B. King's Beale Street Blues Sauce

Barbecue and the blues go together like happy and sad, like fat and sassy, like . . . well, you know the tune. When Riley "Blues Boy" King left Mississippi for Memphis in the '40s, the city was smoking with meat and music. That's still what Memphis visitors crave, and they give it to them at B.B. King's Blues Club on the reborn main drag of the blues, Beale Street. Leander Wilson, the Memphis-born chef, created this dark, thick sauce. "B.B. has given it his taste test," he says, "but to tell you the truth, he's more of a catfish eater."

Makes about 5 cups

1 quart crushed tomatoes
1 cup water
1/2 cup packed brown sugar
1/4 cup diced tomatoes
1/4 cup chili powder
1 tablespoon granulated garlic
1 tablespoon onion powder
1 1/2 teaspoons ground black pepper
5 bay leaves
2 tablespoons chopped onion
2 tablespoons distilled vinegar
2 tablespoons soy sauce
1 tablespoon Worcestershire sauce

- In a large saucepan, combine ingredients.
- Bring to a boil. Reduce heat to low, and simmer for 1 hour. Remove bay leaves. Serve warm.
- Refrigerate unused sauce up to several weeks.

Uses: The strong chili flavor sings out for beef. The club serves it as a table sauce with pork ribs, pork barbecue sandwiches and B.B.'s special Lucille Burgers.

FREDDIE'S HOT HONEY SAUCE

Makes about 7 cups

1 29-ounce can tomato sauce
1/4 cup yellow mustard
2 cups water
1 cup cider vinegar
1 cup honey
1/3 cup packed brown sugar
1 large onion, minced
Juice of 1 lemon
1 tablespoon coarsely ground black pepper
1 tablespoon chili powder
2 to 3 teaspoons red pepper flakes

- In a large saucepan, whisk together the tomato sauce and mustard. Stir in remaining ingredients.
- Bring to a boil. Reduce heat to low, and simmer for 1 hour, stirring occasionally and tasting to adjust seasonings. Serve warm.
- Refrigerate unused sauce up to several weeks.

Uses: As finishing and table sauce on ribs and chicken; also good on hamburgers.

For a Northern city, Cleveland has a respectable number of cooks who know their way around a barbecue pit. The city's annual rib cook-off attracts hordes of people and has no doubt helped cultivate many Ohio palates. Freddie's Southern Style Rib House is neither the biggest nor the most famous barbecue joint in town, but some connoisseurs consider it the best, and he's won countless contests to back them up.

Susan checked out his ribs in Cleveland and liked the sauce so much that she talked owner Freddie Wheeler into giving her some in a Mason jar. "Indian Sauce," he called it.

"My grandmother was Blackfoot," he explained. "She lived to be 107. If she hadn't fallen and hit her head, she'd still be alive today, cooking barbecue."

There's nothing particularly Native American about Freddie's sauce. A son of Troy, Ala., he's been making it since he was 12 and watched his grandmother pick her own vegetables and put up 10 gallons at a time. She'd cook it for hours. That's the secret to good barbecue, he said. "You can't rush it."

Same goes for sauce.

MEAT DOCTORS MIRACLE SAUCE

The remarkable Dr. Pig is unlike any physician we know. Wearing a red-stained gown and a pink plastic snout, he ministers to patients with nothing but a hypodermic needle full of barbecue sauce. Once injected, even D.O.A.'s spring back to life instantly — with pink plastic snouts of their own.

Dr. Pig (real name: Roy Zinn) is the star of the Meat Doctors cooking team's annual skit at the Big Pig Jig, the Georgia state barbecue cook-off. Several of the Doctors work at a hospital in Americus, just up the road from Jimmy Carter's Plains. They took their name from the TV show M*A*S*H (to Hawkeye, military surgeons were just so many meat doctors). They go so far as to wear camouflage and set up their cooking gear in an Army surplus tent.

Is Meat Doctors sauce potent enough to raise the dead? Judges at the Big Pig Jig must have thought so; they named it Georgia's best sauce in 1993.

Makes 6 cups

1 1-pound box light brown sugar
2 cups ketchup
1 cup Worcestershire sauce
3/4 cup honey
1 cup cider or distilled vinegar
6 green onions, trimmed and minced
3 cloves garlic, minced
16 whole cloves
1 bay leaf
1/4 cup dry mustard
1 teaspoon crumbled dry rosemary
1 teaspoon ground oregano
1/2 teaspoon ground black pepper
1/2 teaspoon ground red pepper
1/4 cup (1/2 stick) butter
Juice of 1/2 lemon

- In a large saucepan, combine all ingredients except butter and lemon juice, and simmer over medium-low heat 30 to 45 minutes.
- Reduce heat to low, add butter and lemon juice, and simmer 5 minutes longer.
- Strain, and discard solids. Serve warm.
- Refrigerate unused sauce up to several weeks.

Uses: As a finishing sauce on ribs and pork barbecue. Also good on chicken and hamburgers. Not approved for IV use.

DALLAS MEAT-DRIPPIN' SAUCE

Makes 4 cups

2 cups ketchup (Charlie likes Heinz)
3/4 cup beef drippings
1/2 cup cider vinegar
1/4 cup Worcestershire sauce
1/4 cup lemon juice
1/3 cup packed brown sugar
1 teaspoon onion powder
1/2 teaspoon ground red pepper

- In a large saucepan, combine ingredients, and simmer over low heat 15 minutes.
- Refrigerate unused sauce up to several days; freeze for longer storage.

Uses: Bryan's fanatics pour it over fries, toast and just about anything else nontoxic. But it's best on the beef that brung it — brisket.

There are exactly 24 old school desks to seat diners at the original Sonny Bryan's Smokehouse in Dallas. The lunch crowd usually overflows into the parking lot, where you'll see a truckload of pipefitters next to pinstriped investment bankers gnawing brisket on the trunk of a BMW. Manager Charlie Riddle treats them all the same, whether they're Secret Service agents ordering takeout for George Bush or bodyguards running interference for Sylvester Stallone. Three limos pulled up one time and a man hopped out wanting to clear the dining room for the actor's entourage. "I told him no," Charlie says. "I wasn't going to move my regulars."

Why would swells like Sly flock to a dump like this? We think it's the sauce — smoky, muddy stuff that wouldn't be out of place on a steak. After Sonny died a few years ago, the restaurant franchised and started bottling it. Charlie didn't care much for the taste at first. Says it made him pucker. While he thinks the for-sale sauce has improved, he still prefers the version he mixes daily at the smokehouse. His key ingredient: brisket drippin's.

LBJ's Hail-to-the-Beef Sauce

Presidents have scarfed down barbecue since George Washington was attending pig-pickin's in Virginia. He wrote this entry in his diary in 1769: "Went up to Alexandria for a barbicue." (The Founding Fathers apparently were as confused as we are about how to spell barbecue — or is it bar-b-q?) Despite two centuries of speechifying over smoked meat, it wasn't until the 1960s that a president, Lyndon B. Johnson, hosted a barbecue at the executive mansion. White House chef Henry Haller had never seen a Texas-style barbecue, but that didn't stop him from whipping up a sauce that could have held its own at the LBJ Ranch. We adapted it here.

Makes about 3 cups

1 tablespoon butter
1 large onion, chopped
1 green bell pepper, stemmed, seeded and chopped
3 cloves garlic, minced
2 cups ketchup
1 cup chili sauce
1 cup cider vinegar
1/4 cup Worcestershire sauce
1/4 cup packed brown sugar
12 black peppercorns
1 bay leaf

- In a large saucepan, melt butter. Add onions, bell pepper and garlic, and sauté over medium heat until tender.
- Mix in remaining ingredients. Bring to a boil. Reduce heat to low and simmer for 1 hour.
- Strain, and discard solids. Serve warm. Refrigerate unused sauce up to several weeks.

Uses: As a finishing and table sauce on beef brisket, beef and pork ribs — and recalcitrant members of Congress.

LEXINGTON RED SPLASH

Makes about 2 cups

1 1/2 cups distilled vinegar
2/3 cup ketchup
1/2 cup water
1 tablespoon sugar
1/2 teaspoon ground black pepper
1/2 teaspoon ground red pepper
Pinch or two of red pepper flakes
Salt to taste

- In a small saucepan, combine ingredients, and simmer 15 minutes.
- Store unused sauce indefinitely in a cool, dark place.

Uses: "We don't baste with it. We put it on the meat right before we serve it," says Wayne Monk, who opened Lexington Barbecue in 1962. Some people also use the sauce in coleslaw.

❧

Not to mention lard: William Byrd of Virginia complained in 1728 that "the inhabitants of North Carolina devour so much swine's flesh that it fills them full of gross humours."

❧

Let Memphis and Kansas City squabble over which is America's barbecue capital. Lexington knows the truth. Lexington, N.C. — pop. 16,000 — has 18 barbecue joints, giving it a pork-to-people ratio that must set some kind of record. How seriously does Lexington take barbecue? We asked an executive at Lexington Furniture which restaurant was best, and he looked kind of panicked. "I've got my opinion," he said, "but don't make me tell you. I've got to live in this town."

Lexington Barbecue gave us this recipe (or most of it, at least; they were a little evasive about some of the proportions). It's typical of the thin, puckery sauce they splash on pork barbecue in the Carolina Piedmont.

Savannah-Style Barbecue Sauce

When it comes to barbecue, Savannah is definitely a border town. You can see it in the sauce. Across the river, South Carolinians slap mustard on their pig meat; on the Georgia side, they go for tomatoes. Savannah, ever gracious, does a little of both. The best-known dressing has been served since 1924 at Savannah's Johnny Harris restaurant.

The Johnny Harris people don't go around handing out their sauce recipe, and for good reason; they do a tidy business selling it (see final chapter for information). But Larry Billings, a Savannah native, slipped us this version, which he says was pried loose one night many years ago at the restaurant. "They had this big cook named Fats," Larry says, "and a group of regulars got him drunk." However it happened, we like this sauce's peppery, mustardy bite.

Makes about 7 cups

2 tablespoons chili powder
2 tablespoons ground black pepper
2 teaspoons sugar
1/2 teaspoon salt
4 cups ketchup
1 cup yellow mustard
1/4 cup Worcestershire sauce
2 cups cider vinegar
2 tablespoons butter or margarine
1/4 to 1/2 cup packed brown sugar (optional)

- In a small bowl, combine chili powder, black pepper, sugar and salt.
- In a large saucepan, whisk together ketchup and mustard. Stir in Worcestershire sauce, vinegar and spice mixture, and cook over medium heat 10 minutes. Reduce heat to low, add butter, and simmer until melted.
- Taste. If too tart, stir in brown sugar, and simmer 5 minutes longer. Serve warm.
- Refrigerate unused sauce up to several weeks.

Uses: As a finishing and table sauce for pork and chicken.

BENTLEY'S GOOD-ENOUGH-FOR-LAFAYETTE SAUCE

Makes about 5 cups

2 cups ketchup
2 cups cider vinegar
1 cup water
1/4 cup Worcestershire sauce
3/4 cup packed dark brown sugar
2 tablespoons ground black pepper
Salt and ground red pepper to taste

- In a medium saucepan, combine ingredients, and simmer over medium-low heat 10 to 20 minutes.
- Store unused sauce indefinitely in a cool, dark place.

Uses: As a marinade, finishing or table sauce on pulled pork or chicken. Wouldn't taste bad in a Bloody Mary, either.

Now we know why Lafayette came to America: for the sauce.

We'll explain. Jimmy Bentley, a former Georgia insurance commissioner, comes from a long line of Southern politicians and barbecuers. So long, in fact, that Jimmy still uses the sauce recipe that one of his forebears, Major Charles Abercrombie, served the Marquis de Lafayette when he returned to the States years after fighting with Washington against the British. It's the same sauce Jimmy served Garrison Keillor a few years ago at a public radio fund-raiser in his backyard in Atlanta. Now that's time-tested.

This sauce is typical of Middle Georgia — tomato-based, but sharp and peppery, like something from the Carolinas. "It's better when you let it age," Jimmy says. "I could drink a jigger of it instead of vodka."

Government pork: Years before he became Speaker of the House, Newt Gingrich used to entertain students at West Georgia College with barbecues. They'd dig up his front yard to roast pigs.

Daddy Bob's Sit-Down Cider Sauce

You didn't think you were going to get through this book without a recipe from one of the authors' families, did you? Jim is rather proud of this heirloom, which is as much a part of being an Auchmutey male as a pink complexion and a receding hairline. It originated with his grandfather, Charles Robert Auchmutey Sr. ("Daddy Bob"), a farmer-turned-fireman whose skills as a pitmaster once got him a write-up in the *Saturday Evening Post*. For a 1954 article on "Dixie's Most-Disputed Dish," the magazine sent a writer south to visit some authentic Georgia barbecues. He ended up at the annual feast of the Euharlee Farmers Club, where he met "barbecue chef Robert Auchmutey." (Yes, they called him chef, like he'd attended the Cordon 'Cue or something.) They even ran a picture of him, all purposeful and solemn-faced as he tended pigs and lambs over an open pit. As for condiments, the magazine's writer characterized Georgia barbecue sauces as "tongue-searing." That's funny: We always thought of our sauce as eye-watering and ear-popping. It's vinegary enough to sit you down fast.

Makes 1 1/2 cups

1/2 cup ketchup
1 tablespoon yellow mustard
1 cup cider vinegar
1 teaspoon ground black pepper
Salt to taste

- In a medium saucepan, whisk together ketchup and mustard. Stir in vinegar, pepper and salt. Simmer over medium-low heat 15 minutes.
- Store unused sauce indefinitely in a cool, dark place.

Uses: On pork barbecue and any other meat that needs a wake-up call. Jim's brother, Chuck, once basted Jim's nose with it.

❧

We know how he feels: Journalist Vince Coppola, on a whirlwind tour of Southern barbecue joints for Newsweek, ended his report with a line that got cut: "If I eat one more bite of barbecue, the South will rise again."

❧

MY OLD KENTUCKY SAUCE

Makes about 1 1/2 cups

1 cup cider vinegar
1/4 cup water
1/4 cup coarsely chopped onion
1/4 cup coarsely chopped green bell pepper
1/4 cup coarsely chopped celery
1 teaspoon minced garlic
2 teaspoons whole peppercorns
1 bay leaf
1 cup ketchup
2 tablespoons butter or margarine
2 tablespoons lemon juice
1 tablespoon sugar
1 tablespoon Worcestershire sauce
2 1/2 teaspoons chili powder
2 1/2 teaspoons paprika
1/2 teaspoon dry mustard
1/4 teaspoon Tabasco sauce
1/4 teaspoon liquid smoke
1/4 teaspoon ground red pepper

- In a large saucepan, combine the vinegar, water, onion, bell pepper, celery, garlic, peppercorns and bay leaf. Bring to a boil. Reduce heat to low and simmer for 20 minutes.
- Strain, and discard solids. Return liquid to saucepan. Add remaining ingredients. Stir over medium heat until butter melts. Simmer 5 minutes longer. Serve warm.
- Refrigerate unused sauce up to several weeks.

Uses: As a finishing and table sauce on pork, chicken and mutton.

John Egerton is a distinguished chronicler of the American South, but ever since he wrote *Southern Food*, a definitive survey of the region's cuisine, reporters won't stop asking him about grits and collards. When Leonard's closed its original barbecue pit in Memphis — the one with the strutting neon pig out front — who did *The Wall Street Journal* call for a reaction? "I told them it was roughly equivalent to the fall of Western civilization," John says. "It's tough to sell a serious book when you've got a quote like that on the front of *The Wall Street Journal*."

John has been a dedicated pit follower for years, so naturally we called him to see whether he'd been dabbling with any sauces in his Nashville kitchen. Sure had. It's a complex tomato-and-vinegar number he adapted from Vince Leneave, a cook at a hunting lodge in his hometown of Cadiz, Ky. John uses an incredible 19 ingredients in this recipe and says he left out a couple "to preserve the mystique." That's OK, John; it tastes just right without them.

AVERY ISLAND BARBECUE SAUCE

One of the most common instructions in barbecue recipes is "a couple of dashes of Tabasco sauce." Yet the place it comes from, southern Louisiana, doesn't have much of a barbecue tradition (barbecued crawfish anyone?). We adapted this recipe from the McIlhenney family, which has been making Tabasco on Avery Island since the 1860s. It employs the Holy Trinity of Cajun cooking — celery, onions, bell peppers — as well as Creole mustard and, of course, Tabasco.

Makes about 5 cups

2 tablespoons butter or margarine
1 cup chopped onion
1/2 cup diced celery with leaves
1/4 cup diced green bell pepper
1 tablespoon minced fresh garlic
2 cans (14 1/2 ounces each) tomatoes, undrained
1 can (6 ounces) tomato paste
1/3 cup red wine vinegar
1 cup packed brown sugar
2 lemon slices
1 bay leaf
2 tablespoons Creole mustard
2 tablespoons Worcestershire sauce
2 to 4 tablespoons Tabasco sauce
Salt and pepper to taste

- In a large saucepan, melt butter over medium heat. Add onion, celery, bell pepper and garlic, and sauté 6 to 7 minutes, stirring frequently, until tender.
- Stir in remaining ingredients, breaking up tomatoes with wooden spoon. Bring to a boil.
- Reduce heat to low, cover, and simmer for 30 minutes, stirring occasionally, until sauce is thickened.
- Remove and discard lemon slices and bay leaf. Process in a food processor or blender until smooth. Serve warm.
- Refrigerate unused sauce up to several weeks.

Uses: On ribs, chicken or hamburgers. Or to top a meatloaf.

SYLVIA'S HARLEM BARBECUE SAUCE

Makes about 1 quart

2 large lemons
1 rib celery, finely chopped
1 medium green bell pepper, finely chopped
1/2 large onion, finely chopped
2 cups tomato purée
1 cup hot sauce (Sylvia uses Red Devil)
1 1/2 cups sugar
1/2 teaspoon red pepper flakes

- Squeeze lemons, remove and discard seeds, and slice rinds. Set aside juice and rinds.
- In a blender, purée celery, bell pepper and onion.
- In a saucepan, combine all ingredients, including lemon juice and rinds, over low heat, and simmer 15 to 20 minutes. Remove rinds. Serve warm.
- Refrigerate unused sauce up to several weeks.

Uses: On pork, chicken or hamburgers, but especially good with ribs.

SYLVIA'S OVEN-BARBECUED RIBS

On 6 pounds of pork spareribs, rub 1 tablespoon each salt, black pepper and red pepper flakes. In a glass or plastic container, place ribs in 2 cups distilled vinegar, and refrigerate overnight. Preheat oven to 375 degrees. Transfer ribs to a shallow roasting pan. Roast ribs in oven for 1 1/2 hours. Increase heat to 400 degrees. Turn ribs, and roast 30 minutes longer. Serve with barbecue sauce.

At Sylvia's, the famed soul food restaurant in Harlem, they've been slathering ribs with a bright red, hot-sweet sauce since the early '60s. "It's not Southern-style sauce, per se," says Sylvia Woods, a South Carolina native. "They used a lot more vinegar there. When I first came here, that's how I made mine. Then one of the other chefs and I put our heads together and made a little change."

A pretty big change, actually. They took the vinegar out of the sauce and put it in the marinade. Then to the tomato-based finish they added a bottle of hot sauce, a lot of sugar and a few other signature twists. New Yorkers lapped it up. You can do likewise now that Sylvia markets the sauce nationwide (see the last chapter).

DEACON HUBBARD'S WHEAT STREET MOP

There is an unwritten Eleventh Commandment at the Wheat Street Baptist Church in Atlanta's Martin Luther King Jr. historic district: Thou shalt not baste with barbecue sauce. That tomato stuff is fine for the table, but to see spareribs through fire and brimstone, you need to bless them with something thin and tart. Something like this mop that members Robert Hughey and James Rowland Jr. use when they cook for the board of ushers. They actually brush it on with a short-handled mop. The recipe comes from their mentor, the late Deacon Mark Hubbard, who had a standard response when people asked him why he didn't market his barbecue skills: "I'm rich when I make my friends happy."

Somebody say amen.

Makes 2 1/2 cups

1 cup Worcestershire sauce
1 tablespoon margarine
1 tablespoon ketchup
1 cup cider vinegar
1/4 cup water
1/2 teaspoon ground black pepper
1/2 teaspoon paprika
Salt to taste

- In a small saucepan, combine Worcestershire sauce and margarine over medium-high heat, and simmer until margarine is melted.
- Add remaining ingredients. Bring to a boil. Remove from heat and serve warm.
- Refrigerate unused baste up to several weeks.

THE DEACON HAD A BARBECUE SAUCE, TOO.

Makes about 3 1/2 cups

1/4 cup (1/2 stick) butter or margarine
1/4 cup chopped onion
1 28-ounce can whole tomatoes with juice
1 cup Worcestershire sauce
1 cup distilled or cider vinegar
1/2 tablespoon sugar
1/2 teaspoon paprika
1/2 teaspoon dry mustard
1/4 teaspoon ground black pepper
1/4 teaspoon salt

1/8 teaspoon ground red pepper
1/2 lemon
1/3 cup tomato paste

- In a large saucepan, melt butter over medium heat. Add onion and sauté until tender. Add all remaining ingredients, except lemon and tomato paste. Bring to a boil.
- Squeeze lemon juice into sauce, then drop in lemon half. Reduce heat to low, and simmer for 30 to 45 minutes.
- Remove lemon, let cool, and squeeze again. Discard lemon.
- Strain solids, and return sauce to pot.
- Stir in tomato paste, and cook, stirring, 5 minutes longer.
- Refrigerate unused sauce up to several weeks.

Uses: Brush the basting sauce on ribs, fresh ham or chicken as it cooks. After removing meat from the grill, brush with barbecue sauce. The ribs always come between slices of white bread. It's probably in the Bible somewhere.

When clowns collide: In the late '80s Larry Harmon, a.k.a. Bozo the Clown, sued Bozo's Barbecue in Mason, Tenn., for trademark infringement. A court ruled against him, saying Bozo's had been in business longer. "Why the clown should have a lock on it I don't understand," said writer and barbecue lover Shelby Foote.

SWINE LAKE BALLET SAUCE

Roll over, Tchaikovsky, they're making pig meat out of your masterpiece in Mississippi. In the great tradition of silly cook-off team names, the Swine Lake Ballet may have come up with the silliest. To make matters sillier, this group of lawyers and insurance agents from Corinth, Miss., has been known to don pink tutus to entertain contest judges. In spite of this stomach-challenging spectacle, they have won quite a few prizes.

There's nothing silly about Swine Lake Ballet Sauce. Dark as Mississippi mud, it's sneaky-hot (mustard), a little sweet (brown sugar) and positively sinus-opening (vinegar, lots of vinegar). Here's how team member Jon Hill makes it.

Makes about 2 cups

1 cup yellow mustard
1 cup cider vinegar
2/3 cup packed brown sugar
3 tablespoons paprika
1 heaping tablespoon chili powder
1 teaspoon ground red pepper
1 teaspoon white pepper
1 teaspoon MSG (optional)

- In a medium saucepan, combine ingredients over medium-low heat, and simmer 10 to 15 minutes. Serve warm.
- Refrigerate unused sauce up to several weeks.

Uses: As a marinade, baste and table sauce for pork or poultry. Be careful: It doesn't wash out of tutus.

CAROLINA PIG-PICKIN' SAUCE

Makes about 1 quart

1 quart cider vinegar
1/4 cup packed brown sugar
3 tablespoons salt, or to taste
1 tablespoon red pepper flakes
1 1/2 teaspoons ground red pepper
1 teaspoon ground black pepper

- In a large container, combine ingredients. Let stand at least 4 hours.
- Store unused sauce indefinitely in a cool, dark place.

Uses: On pulled pork barbecue sandwiches.

America's oldest barbecue sauce strikes a lot of people as odd because it doesn't use tomatoes. Eastern Carolinians can get quite defensive about the spiced vinegar they use at pig-pickin's, as they call whole-hog roasts. Journalists like Tom Wicker and Charles Kuralt — both natives — seem to feel it their birthright to defend local barbecue customs. We adapted this recipe from another Carolina native, Atlanta food consultant Elaine Harvell, who researched Tar Heel sauces for the North Carolina Pork Producers Association.

Cruel and unusual punishment: Police in 1957 arrested a night prowler at Scott's Barbecue in Goldsboro, N.C. Denied a shower, he was pink and pickled by morning — he'd been hiding in a vat of peppered vinegar sauce.

FOOLING WITH FRUIT

When you think about it, almost all barbecue sauces are fruit-based. The tomato, after all, is a fruit, and vinegar is nothing but apple juice with an attitude. Putting fruit sauce on meat is an idea as old as Thanksgiving turkey with cranberries.

Some of the most creative saucemaking in America today involves fruit. It's showing up in a wide range of salsas and chutneys and ketchups. Fruit seems particularly sympathetic to smoked meat. At the American Royal cook-off in Kansas City, where they have a whole category for fruit sauces, they've seen them with raspberries, apricot jam, apple butter — just about anything that falls out of a pantry or produce bin.

Fruit-bases tend to fall into two types: sweet finishing sauces and glazes for pork and beef, and tropical citrus sauces and marinades for seafood and chicken. They add color to the table and personality to the meat.

But not everything works. John Willingham, a Memphis barbecue man, warned us about the worst sauce he'd ever tasted. "It was in Missouri," he said. "I think it had persimmons in it. I was so puckered I couldn't get a rib in my mouth."

There are no persimmons in this chapter. Promise.

BLACKBERRY-CHAMBORD BARBECUE SAUCE

When we first saw a version of this recipe, we didn't know what to make of it. Blackberries? Chambord liqueur? Do you put it on meat or melons? Much to our delight, the seemingly frou-frou ingredients melded into something any backyard barbe-cuer would be pleased to slap on a carcass. It's quite different, as fiery as it is fruity. We adapted the recipe from the Colorado Beef Council and the Colorado Restaurant Association.

Makes about 5 cups

2 to 3 cups fresh blackberries, or 1 12- or 16-ounce package frozen loose-pack blackberries, thawed
2 cups beef broth
2 cups tomato sauce
2/3 cup packed brown sugar
1 small onion, minced
2 tablespoons Chambord liqueur
2 tablespoons barbecue seasoning
1 tablespoon hot pepper sauce
2 teaspoons ground red pepper
1 teaspoon onion powder
1/2 teaspoon allspice
1/2 teaspoon ground star anise or five-spice powder

• In a blender or food processor, purée the berries. Pour into a large saucepan along with remaining ingredients.
• Bring to a boil. Reduce heat to low, and simmer, uncovered, for 15 to 20 minutes.
• Refrigerate unused sauce up to a few days, or freeze.

Uses: As a finishing and table sauce for chicken, pork ribs or beef brisket. It's a tad hot for honeydew.

BANANA MOLASSES BETTER-THAN-KETCHUP

Makes about 5 cups

1 cup cider vinegar
1 cup water
3 ripe bananas, peeled and chopped
1/2 cup minced onion
1/3 cup raisins (dark or golden)
1/3 cup molasses
1/3 cup tomato paste
1/4 cup honey
1/4 cup dark rum
1 tablespoon minced garlic
1 jalapeño pepper, seeded and minced
1 teaspoon salt
1/2 teaspoon ground cinnamon
1/2 teaspoon red pepper flakes
1/4 teaspoon ground red pepper
1/8 teaspoon ground nutmeg
1/8 teaspoon ground cloves

- In a saucepan, combine all ingredients over medium heat.
- Bring to a boil. Reduce heat to low, and simmer, uncovered, for 20 to 30 minutes, stirring frequently, or until syrupy.
- Transfer mixture to a blender or food processor fitted with a steel blade; purée until smooth.
- Refrigerate unused sauce up to 2 weeks.

Uses: As a table sauce for dipping grilled shrimp, topping hamburgers or most any meat, chicken or seafood.

Steven Raichlen, an award-winning cookbook author and South Florida food expert, calls this ketchup. That's like calling Jack Daniel's corn whiskey. We think you'll agree that the K word doesn't do justice to our version of Steven's recipe, which he included in his cookbook *Miami Spice.*

Apple City Sauce

Being a vegetarian, Johnny Appleseed probably didn't know the pleasures of barbecued pork butt. We say *probably* because we've known a few vegetarians who backslid from time to time when confronted by the perfume of the pit. Whether Johnny ever did, he contributed mightily to America's barbecue heritage if only through the trees he planted across the Midwest. Apple squeezings go great on smoked meat, and no one has made better use of them than the Apple City cook-off team of Murphysboro, Ill.

Bar owner Mike Mills started the crew in 1989 with his friend Pat Burke. They went on to win an unprecedented three grand prizes in the Memphis in May world championship. Their secret? Apples, of course. Any apples will do, but Mike believes ribs taste best with Golden Delicious. Somewhere, Johnny Appleseed is salivating.

Makes 2 cups

1 cup ketchup
1/4 cup soy sauce
1/4 cup cider vinegar
1/4 cup apple juice
2 tablespoons Worcestershire sauce
1/4 medium onion, finely grated
2 teaspoons grated green bell pepper
3/4 teaspoon granulated garlic
3/4 teaspoon ground white pepper
Sugar to taste
1/4 apple, peeled and grated (preferably Golden Delicious)

- In a medium saucepan, combine all ingredients except apple, and simmer over low heat 5 to 10 minutes.
- Add grated apple, and simmer 5 minutes longer. Refrigerate unused sauce for up to 1 week.

Uses: As a finishing and table sauce with any kind of pork, especially ribs. Mike starts them with Apple City's dry rub:

Magic Dust Rub

Makes about 1/2 cup

2 1/2 tablespoons coarsely ground black pepper
2 1/2 tablespoons paprika
1 1/2 tablespoons chili powder
1 1/2 teaspoons celery salt
1 1/4 teaspoons ground red pepper
1 1/4 teaspoons granulated garlic
3/4 teaspoon dry mustard
1/8 teaspoon ground cinnamon

It all comes together in

Apple City Pork Ribs

Sprinkle ribs with Magic Dust, and cook in smoker for 5 1/2 to 6 1/2 hours over apple wood, misting the meat several times with apple juice. Sprinkle with Magic Dust another two or three times during cooking. About 20 minutes before taking off the fire, dab ribs with sauce, being careful not to brush off rub.

Bad to the bone: If you could get trichinosis from puns, the barbecue cook-off circuit would be doubled over with cramps. Here are some rancidly cute names we've seen: Pepto Porkers, Oink, Cackle & Moo, Hogaholics, Pot-Bellied Porkers, Super Swine Sizzlers, Porkinators, Hog Rock Cafe, WGAS and (goodness gracious) Great Boars of Fire.

Georgia Peach Marinade and Glaze

Don't pour this peach glaze over ice cream! It's intended for pork, and what a fine match they are. The recipe comes from the Georgia Peach Commission.

Marinade

Makes about 2/3 cup

1/3 cup low-sodium soy sauce
2 tablespoons lemon juice
1 tablespoon vegetable oil
1 tablespoon peach preserves
1 clove garlic, minced
2 teaspoons minced fresh ginger, or 1 teaspoon powdered ginger

Glaze

Makes about 1 1/4 cups

1 cup finely chopped fresh or frozen peaches (thawed, with juice)
2 tablespoons lemon juice
2 tablespoons sugar
1 tablespoon low-sodium soy sauce
1 1/2 teaspoons cornstarch
1 clove garlic, minced
1 teaspoon minced fresh ginger, or 1/2 teaspoon powdered ginger

- In a glass or plastic container large enough to hold meat, combine marinade ingredients.
- In a small saucepan, mix glaze ingredients. Bring to a boil. Reduce heat to low, and simmer for 3 to 5 minutes or until thickened and bubbly.
- Unused marinade will keep indefinitely in refrigerator. Unused glaze may be refrigerated up to several days.

Uses: On pork chops or pork tenderloins, or try this:

Pork Kebabs

Makes 6 servings

- Place 1 1/2 pounds of pork tenderloin, cut into 1-inch cubes, in Peach Marinade. Stir to coat. Cover, and refrigerate 4 to 6 hours or overnight.
- Drain pork, and discard marinade. On 6 skewers, arrange cubes of pork, squares of red or green bell pepper, chunks of onion and — if they are in season — wedges of fresh peaches.
- Place kebabs on grill or under broiler 4 to 6 inches from heat source. Brush with glaze.
- Cook 15 to 20 minutes or until meat is no longer pink and vegetables are crisp and tender, turning once, and basting frequently with glaze.
- Reheat any leftover glaze 1 to 2 minutes in the microwave, and serve on the side.

Piggy B. Goode: Something about Georgia makes people want to sing about barbecue. One of the first blues men to record in the '20s was Atlanta's "Barbecue Bob" Hicks. More recently, there have been two rock bands: Mighty Fine Slabs from Atlanta and the Barbecue Killers from Athens.

MAUI MANGO-GINGER SAUCE

Hawaiians are used to dipping roast pig in chili-pepper water at luaus and dousing fish or Korean short ribs with a teriyaki marinade before slapping them onto their backyard hibachis. But Mark Ellman, chef at Avalon Restaurant in Lahaina, Maui, has other ideas about barbecue sauce. A founder of Hawaii Regional Cuisine — a group of chefs out to prove that there's more to their state's food than poi or pineapple — the L.A. transplant combines the island's best with his own creative flourishes in this fiery-sweet condiment. "We serve it with seared mahi-mahi on a bed of polenta, surrounded with a spicy garlic spinach," he says. For more recipes from Mark and other creative Hawaiian chefs, check out their cookbook, *The New Cuisine of Hawaii*.

Makes about 1 quart

1/4 cup olive oil
1 cup minced Maui (or other) onion
1 cup peeled and minced fresh ginger
2 to 3 jalapeño peppers, stemmed, seeded and minced
Salt and coarsely ground black pepper to taste
1 cup red wine vinegar
1 cup Maui raw sugar (or 1/2 cup each brown sugar
* and granulated sugar)*
1 cup Maui (or other) mango purée
1/2 cup mango chutney
1 cup ketchup
1 cup tomato purée
1/2 cup chopped cilantro
1/4 cup Worcestershire sauce

- In a large, heavy saucepan, heat oil over medium heat.
- Add onion, ginger and jalapeño peppers, and sauté until tender. Season with salt and pepper.
- Add vinegar, sugar, mango purée and chutney. Simmer over low heat 10 minutes.
- Add ketchup, tomato purée, cilantro and Worcestershire sauce. Simmer over low heat 1 hour.
- Purée, and press through a strainer into a container.
- Refrigerate unused sauce up to several days (up to several weeks if you omit cilantro).

Uses: As a finishing and table sauce for seafood, chicken or pork.

Low-Sodium Orange-Clove Sauce

Makes about 6 cups

6 medium onions, peeled and quartered
2 heads garlic, broken into cloves, peeled
1 12-ounce can orange juice concentrate
3 cups water
1 1/2 cups dry white wine
1/2 cup red wine vinegar
1/3 cup powdered fructose (available at health food
    stores; sugar or honey may be substituted)
1 1/2 teaspoons ground cloves
1 teaspoon ground red pepper

- In a large saucepan, combine onion, garlic, orange juice, water, wine and vinegar.
- Bring to a boil. Reduce heat to low, and simmer, uncovered, for 45 minutes or until onions and garlic are very soft.
- In a blender or food processor fitted with a steel blade, purée mixture in batches until smooth, then return to saucepan.
- Add fructose, cloves and red pepper. Cook over low heat 30 minutes. (For a smoother, thicker sauce, stir in a little cornstarch mixed with water and continue to cook until it thickens.)
- Refrigerate unused sauce up to 1 week, or freeze.

Uses: As a baste for poultry, seafood and lamb. Also can be used as a table sauce. For vegetables, seafood and white meats, mix baste with yogurt or sour cream. For red meats, use ketchup.

Brian Koba isn't your typical barbecuer. Ask him for a trim, and he's as likely to go for your bangs as your brisket. Brian is a hairstylist, an award-winning one, but there's something about the cultural breezes of Seattle that turns half the population into good cooks. Brian has come up with a line of sauces that combine Asian flavors with traditional American barbecue. What's more, they're low-sodium. "The first people to pick them up were the health-conscious," he says. "But I'm no vegetarian. I love my beef."

This is our interpretation of one of Brian's most popular fusions, which uses a purée of slow-simmered onions and garlic as its flavor base. Though it bears virtually no resemblance to conventional sauce, it's a surprisingly flavorful healthy alternative. To try his other sauces, see final chapter for mail-order information.

Quit the day job, Brian.

TODD'S SWEET-TOOTH CHERRY SAUCE

Todd Goodew grew up in a restaurant family and cooked barbecue at an early age. But when he started competing on the cook-off circuit, the sauces quickly bored him. Too similar. Then he discovered fruit-based sauces. "They're the wave of the future," he says. "Kids just love them on hamburgers; it's like eating candy." We felt that way about this cherry sauce (depending on your sweet tooth, you may want to reduce the brown sugar). Todd markets several sauces out of Redmond, Ore., under the Rocky Mountain label. (For ordering information, see final chapter.)

Makes 3 cups

1 cup cherry spreadable fruit
1 cup ketchup
1 cup packed brown sugar
3 to 5 tablespoons yellow mustard
2 tablespoons lemon juice
1/2 teaspoon liquid smoke

- In a medium saucepan, combine ingredients, and simmer over low heat 10 to 15 minutes or until brown sugar is melted.
- Press sauce through a medium-mesh sieve into a container to remove cherry skins.
- Refrigerate unused sauce up to several weeks.

Uses: As a finishing and table sauce with pork and hamburgers.

PLUM CHUTNEY BARBECUE SAUCE

Makes about 3 cups

1 cup chopped red onion
1 green bell pepper, cored, seeded and chopped
1 orange, peeled, sectioned and chopped (some peel left
on, if desired)
1 large tomato, peeled, cored and chopped
2 cloves garlic, chopped
1/2 cup lime juice
1 1/2 cups plum jam or preserves
1 tablespoon pumpkin pie spice

- In a medium saucepan, combine onion, green pepper, orange, tomato, garlic and lime juice.
- Bring to a boil. Reduce heat to low, and simmer, uncovered, for 45 minutes.
- Purée until nearly smooth in a blender or food processor.
- Stir in plum jam and pie spice. Simmer over low heat 15 minutes, stirring often. Serve warm.
- Refrigerate unused sauce up to several weeks. It may be necessary to slightly reheat before serving to thin.

Uses: Brush over grilled pork, ham or chicken during the last few minutes of cooking.

Barbecue sauces don't usually boast of their fresh ingredients — most, after all, are proud conglomerations of pantry staples — but this one's a notable exception. *Cincinnati Post* food editor Joyce Rosencrans adapted it years ago from a press release, and its fresh, spicy taste still stands out in her memory. "If you buy a small, inexpensive, boneless ham from the supermarket — the kind that's usually bland and tasteless — smoke it over applewood chips and brush some of this over it afterward, it tastes like something special."

We found that it had the same effect on cheap chicken wings.

Papaya-Ginger Barbecue Sauce

Chef Tony Modera develops recipes for the exotic produce grown and distributed by Brooks Tropicals of Homestead, Fla. He likes to baste chicken with this fresh, light, easy sauce that makes use of some of his company's top sellers. It's infinitely versatile. "It can be made as a marinade by adding a little soy sauce or vinegar," he says. "To use it as a finishing sauce, you might add some brown sugar or honey." And if you don't mind the extra calories, a little olive oil or vegetable oil wouldn't hurt, either.

Makes about 1 1/4 cups

3/4 cup orange juice
1/2 papaya, peeled, seeded and sliced
2 tablespoons grated fresh ginger
2 tablespoons honey (optional)
1 1/2 teaspoons soy sauce (optional)
1 1/2 teaspoons rice vinegar (optional)
1/2 teaspoon hot chili oil (optional)

- In a blender or food processor fitted with a steel blade, combine ingredients, and purée until smooth.
- Refrigerate unused sauce up to several days.

Variation: In place of the optional ingredients, substitute 2 tablespoons olive or vegetable oil, 1 tablespoon Dijon mustard and 1 tablespoon lemon juice.

Uses: Baste chicken during the last 10 minutes on the grill. Or baste pork, shrimp, scallops or other seafood.

BERRY BERRY HOT GLAZE

Makes 1 3/4 cups

1 cup fresh cranberries
1 cup water
1/2 cup raspberry jam
1/4 cup raspberry vinegar
1 jalapeño pepper, stemmed, seeded and minced
1/2 teaspoon coarsely ground black pepper
1/4 teaspoon ground red pepper
1/4 teaspoon salt

- In a small saucepan, combine cranberries and water, and cook over medium-high heat 5 minutes, or until the berries pop.
- Blend in the jam and vinegar.
- Transfer to a blender or food processor fitted with a steel blade. Add jalapeño, black pepper, red pepper and salt. Purée until smooth.
- Refrigerate unused glaze up to 1 week, or freeze.

Uses: As a glaze and a dipping sauce for chicken or pork (it's especially good with pork chops). Baste meat during the last few minutes of cooking. Reheat extra sauce, and offer on the side.

This one is ours. We wanted a bright red sauce that'd be pretty in a picture. So we started mixing cranberries and raspberries and red fingernail polish (just kidding) and soon had a pot of something almost as photogenic as Cindy Crawford's lips — sweet and hot (the sauce, that is) and as tasty as it is attractive. Why ask why?

CRESCENT DRAGONWAGON'S BLUEBERRY SAUCE

Nobody paid much attention to Arkansas cuisine until Bill Clinton was elected president. Then for a brief time it seemed everyone was curious. By some accounts, the best discovery was Crescent Dragonwagon's "Nouveau 'Zarks" cuisine, an imaginative melding of Ozarks ingredients and French techniques that she serves at the Dairy Hollow House in Eureka Springs. When it's blueberry season, Crescent offers a chicken wing appetizer glazed with a fresh-tasting sauce much like this. We found it as interesting as her name.

Makes about 2 cups

2 tablespoons butter
3/4 cup chopped celery
3/4 cup chopped onion
3/4 cup chopped green bell pepper
1/2 cup minced carrot
1 clove garlic, minced
1 quart fresh or frozen blueberries (thawed)
1/2 cup raspberry or cider vinegar
1/3 cup honey
1 tablespoon molasses
1 1/2 teaspoons paprika
3/4 teaspoon salt
3/4 teaspoon ground black pepper
1/2 teaspoon ground cinnamon
1/8 teaspoon ground nutmeg
1/8 teaspoon dry mustard
1/8 teaspoon ground cloves
1/8 teaspoon celery seed
1/8 teaspoon powdered ginger
1/8 teaspoon ground red pepper

- In a large saucepan, melt butter over low heat. Add celery, onion, bell pepper, carrot and garlic. Sauté until vegetables are tender but not browned.
- Transfer to a blender, add blueberries, and purée until smooth.
- Return mixture to the saucepan. Add remaining ingredients.
- Simmer over medium-low heat 10 to 15 minutes, or until the mixture is slightly thickened.

- While still hot, press sauce through a sieve.
- Refrigerate unused sauce up to 2 weeks, or freeze.

Uses: As a baste for chicken, turkey, quail, shrimp or pork. Crescent suggests marinating chicken wings in the following mixture 3 to 8 hours before grilling or baking in the oven; then brushing with the blueberry sauce during the last 20 minutes of cooking.

MARINADE FOR WINGS

1/2 cup raspberry or other fruit vinegar
2 tablespoons honey
2 tablespoons tamari sauce
1 tablespoon minced garlic
1 tablespoon minced fresh ginger
1 teaspoon Pickapeppa or Worcestershire sauce
1/2 teaspoon coarse salt
1/2 teaspoon cracked black pepper
Hot pepper sauce to taste

- In a large container, combine ingredients.
- Refrigerate unused marinade indefinitely.

Presidential pork: The best-known barbecue joint in Arkansas might be McClard's of Hot Springs. Not only did it help put the pudge on local boy Bill Clinton, but it was featured for several years on network TV. It was pictured in the opening montage of Evening Shade and was a model for Ossie Davis' barbecue place in the show.

Mark Miller's Tamarind Chipotle Sauce

Most Americans have tried tamarind; they just don't realize it. The sour brown pulp contained in its fuzzy pods helps flavor Worcestershire sauce and other condiments, including some barbecue sauces. The fruit plays a far more prominent role in Latin and Asian cuisines, where it's sipped as a fruit drink or stirred into curry or stew.

Chef Mark Miller likes to use tamarind at his Southwest-chic restaurants, the Coyote Cafe in Santa Fe, N.M., and Red Sage in Washington, D.C. He concocted this intriguing sauce one evening while cooking ribs for an outdoor barbecue, and it's been a favorite ever since. A version appears in his *The Great Chile Book*. He uses tamarind in convenient paste form, but if all you can find is blocks of compressed tamarind you can still make it — just be advised that straining out the rock-hard seeds and tough fibers is a bit of a workout. Look for either form of tamarind in Latin, Indian or other Asian markets. Mark tempers the tartness with some brown sugar, then heats it up with smoky chipotle peppers.

Makes about 1 1/4 cups

1 cup water (more, if needed)
7 or 8 ounces tamarind paste or compressed tamarind
1/4 to 1/3 cup packed brown sugar
1 or 2 cloves garlic, minced (roast first if desired)
1 canned chipotle chili in adobo sauce
Lime juice to taste (optional)

- In a medium saucepan, combine water and tamarind. Heat gently, stirring until pulp has dissolved. Add a little more water if it becomes too dry.
- Press mixture through a sieve into a bowl to strain out hard seeds and fibers.
- Place pulp in a blender and purée with 1/4 cup of brown sugar, garlic and chili.
- Taste to adjust seasoning, adding a little more sugar if it seems too tart, or a little more adobo sauce if you want more heat. Add a little lime juice if desired. Serve slightly warmed.
- Refrigerate unused sauce up to several weeks.

Uses: As a baste and finishing sauce on pork, chicken, shrimp and other seafood.

LIME-CILANTRO MARINADE

Makes about 1 cup

1/3 cup fresh lime juice
2 teaspoons coarsely grated lime peel
1/4 cup olive oil
2 cloves garlic, minced
1/3 cup chopped fresh cilantro
1 1/2 teaspoons hot pepper sauce
1 1/2 teaspoons dried oregano
3/4 teaspoon salt
1/4 teaspoon coarsely ground black pepper

- In a large, shallow glass baking dish, combine ingredients.
- Refrigerate unused marinade up to several days.

Uses: As a marinade for chicken, steaks, fish or shrimp (enough for about 2 pounds). Marinate at least 30 minutes. Baste with leftover marinade. If cooking in the oven, serve with pan drippings.

Some marinades sound great on paper but taste like nothing after the meat's been cooked. Not this one. Adapted from a National Chicken Cooking Contest finalist, this marinade has a refreshingly tart, summery flavor that will make you glad you went to the trouble to grate that lime peel.

New World Grapefruit Barbecue Sauce

No, Columbus didn't discover this sauce. "New World" is the term its creator, Allen Susser of Chef Allen's in North Miami Beach, uses to describe his cooking, which makes heavy use of local tropical ingredients. It won him the 1994 James Beard Award for best American chef in the Southeast. In his book, *New World Cuisine,* Allen pairs a clean-tasting citrus sauce with pompano. We used our version on grouper and chicken.

Makes about 2 cups

Zest (colored part of peel) and juice of 2 large grapefruits
1 cup sugar
1 cup water
1/4 cup Asian chili-garlic sauce (available in Oriental markets)
2 tablespoons soy sauce
2 tablespoons honey
2 tablespoons lime juice

- Blanch the grapefruit zest twice to remove bitterness: In a small saucepan, place the zest and cover with cold water. Bring to a boil. Drain the zest, return to the saucepan and repeat process.
- Combine blanched zest in the saucepan with the sugar and 1 cup of water. Over medium heat, bring the mixture to a simmer and cook for about 30 minutes, or until reduced to about 1/2 cup.
- Heat the grapefruit juice and add to the grapefruit syrup. (Heating the juice first will prevent the syrup from crystallizing, although if you forget and add it cold, don't panic — it will liquefy as it cooks.)
- Add remaining ingredients. Simmer about 20 minutes longer, or until syrupy. Remove from heat and let cool.
- Refrigerate unused sauce up to 2 weeks.

Uses: As a baste and table sauce for chicken or seafood. Also good with pork tenderloin.

PEAR-MUSTARD SAUCE

Makes 3/4 cup

1 16-ounce can pears in heavy syrup, drained
3 tablespoons syrup reserved from can
1 tablespoon Dijon mustard
1 tablespoon cider vinegar
2 teaspoons honey
1/4 teaspoon Tabasco sauce
1/4 teaspoon ground black pepper
1/4 teaspoon salt

- In a blender or food processor fitted with a steel blade, purée pears until smooth.
- Blend in remaining ingredients. Pour into a saucepan, and heat just until warm.
- Refrigerate unused sauce up to several weeks.

Uses: As a table sauce for grilled sausage, pork chops or smoked turkey.

When we first heard of this one, we wondered whether it was flavor fusion or flavor confusion. But no combination is too bizarre when it comes to sauce, so we gave it a try. Good thing. More pear than mustard, it's refreshing and unusual.

FRUIT-AND-SPICE BARBECUE SAUCE

Let's face it: A lot of people doctor bottled barbecue sauces and pass them off as their own. No need to be shy about it. One of America's biggest barbecue nuts freely admits to it. Roy Blount Jr. says he starts out with a bottled sauce from the last place he had good barbecue, then adds what's left in the bottle he got from the place before that. "I know that you get muddy colors from mixing different colors of paint injudiciously, but I don't know that there is anything wrong about muddy barbecue sauce," Roy told us. "In fact, maybe a little mud or red clay wouldn't be too bad."

Thanks, Roy. But it's so hard to find good mud in the store, we thought we'd go with this recipe from Cleveland food consultant John Faenza instead. It went over big at a cooking class he taught, which happened to be attended by a friend of Susan's, who in turn shared it with us.

Makes about 3 1/2 cups

2 cups tomato-based barbecue sauce (John uses Open Pit)
1/4 cup molasses
1/4 cup packed brown sugar
1/4 cup apricot preserves
1/4 cup honey
1/4 cup orange juice concentrate
1/4 cup orange marmalade
3 tablespoons cider vinegar
2 tablespoons Worcestershire sauce
1 tablespoon five-spice powder
1 tablespoon red pepper flakes

- In a saucepan, combine ingredients, and simmer over low heat 10 to 15 minutes.
- Refrigerate unused sauce up to several weeks.

Uses: As a baste, finishing sauce or table sauce for pork, beef or chicken.

MORE IDEAS FOR DOCTORING SAUCE

To your favorite brand, add a taste of:

Florida: undiluted fruit juice concentrate (lemonade, limeade, orange or grapefruit juice).

Georgia: peach preserves (puréed in a blender with a shot of bourbon).

Louisiana: sautéed green pepper, celery and onion; Tabasco sauce and Cajun seasoning.

New England: jellied cranberry sauce and a little maple syrup or molasses, heated to melt the cranberry sauce.

New Mexico: beer, lime juice, a dash each of cumin and chili powder and some chopped cilantro.

North Carolina: cider vinegar and lots of red pepper flakes and ground black pepper.

Seattle: extra-strong espresso.

Texas: red pepper jelly (heated until melted), or bottled Mexican salsa (puréed in a blender).

Wrigley Field: yellow mustard and sweet pickle relish.

Asia: bottled hoisin sauce, soy sauce, sesame oil and fresh or powdered ginger.

The Caribbean: pineapple juice, dark rum, brown sugar and Pickapeppa sauce.

India: mango chutney and a little curry powder (puréed in a blender and heated to meld flavors).

Italy: bottled Italian dressing.

Mexico: prepared Mexican mole sauce (available in Latin markets), heated and stirred until blended.

Big Red: America's best-selling barbecue sauce, by far, is Kraft. It has a third of the market, according to Packaged Facts. The No. 2 and No. 3 brands, Bull's-Eye and K.C. Masterpiece, have less market share combined.

ANYTHING GOES

*P*eople have put some pretty strange things in barbecue sauce over the years. We've heard of recipes with cactus juice, watermelon rind, licorice, Reese's Peanut Butter Cups, even cough syrup. No joke. Vince Staten, coauthor of the book *Real Barbecue,* once concocted something called "Mr. Vince's Hacking Sauce" that contained half a teaspoon of Terpin hydrate D-M cough syrup. He entered it in a contest and finished ahead of some rather famous labels. It was the only sauce, Vince says, "that could tinge your palate while soothing your throat."

Well, we made a rule when we started this cookbook: No ingredients would come from a pharmacy. Just about anything else is fair game, from maple syrup to juniper berries to sweet potatoes.

We've noticed that saucemakers seem particularly fond of pouring their favorite beverages in their barbecue dressings. Beer, bourbon, Coke, tequila — if they can sip it, they sauce it. It reminds us of an informal basting recipe related by Thelma Balfour of the Memphis in May cook-off. "They'll take a couple of six-packs and say, 'One can for me, one for the pig. Two cans for me, one for the pig. Three cans for me, one for the pig ...'"

Sounds like those guys could use our coffee sauce.

REMUS'S AFRICAN GROUNDNUT SAUCE

It all started in 1984. Ardie Davis, a mild-mannered Kansan, was reading *Roadfood* by Jane and Michael Stern when their descriptions of barbecue joints started his motor running. He didn't have the money to visit all those places, so he did the next best thing: He wrote and asked the restaurants for barbecue sauce. Twenty-five or so jars came back in the mail. Ardie gathered friends in his backyard to grade the flavors, and the first Diddy-Wa-Diddy sauce contest was joined.

The annual event continues today as the American Royal International Barbecue Sauce Contest. Saucemakers from across the country compete in 16 categories from best fruit-base to best sauce label. And Ardie is still there, wearing a bowler and a necklace of rib bones, as he administers an oath to contest judges. Remus Powers, he calls his barbecue alter ego.

Remus is quite the connoisseur. He keeps dozens of sauces in the basement — his sauce cellar — sampling no more at one

Makes about 9 cups

2 tablespoons canola or vegetable oil
1 medium onion, finely chopped
1 tablespoon mashed smoke-roasted garlic (see Page 68 for instructions) or 4 cloves garlic, minced, if short on time
1 tablespoon red pepper flakes, or to taste
5 cups canned tomato sauce
1 cup orange juice
1 cup distilled vinegar
1 cup crunchy or smooth peanut butter (Remus prefers Jif)
1/2 cup cooked mashed sweet potato
2 tablespoons tamarind pulp (see Page 56) or lime juice

- In a large saucepan, heat oil over medium heat. Add onion, garlic and red pepper flakes, and sauté until onion is tender.
- Add remaining ingredients. Bring to a boil. Reduce heat to medium low, and simmer for 5 to 10 minutes, stirring with a wooden spoon. Serve warm.
- Refrigerate unused sauce up to 1 week.

Uses: As a table sauce with smoked or grilled chicken breast, pork ribs or beef brisket.

The Remus Powers oath: "I do solemnly swear to objectively and subjectively evaluate each Barbecue Sauce that is presented to my eyes, my nose and my palate. I accept my duty ... so that truth, justice, excellence in Barbecue and the American Way of Life may be strengthened and preserved forever."

time than will fit in a shelf of the refrigerator door. (That's all his wife will allow.) He evaluates the new vintages with his special ceramic spoon, first sniffing, then sipping, then pouring it on whatever's handy — meat, cheese, cantaloupe. "The more I taste, the more I prefer the tangy sauces," he says. "I'm like a wine drinker going from sweet to dry."

An adventurous palate like Remus's won't settle for the same old sauce. This recipe was inspired by his first taste of Groundnut Stew, a West African medley of peanuts, meat, vegetables and spices. He merged it with a Thai-style peanut sauce and came up with this unusual orange condiment that's so tasty it almost makes meat unnecessary.

Death Row Bourbon Sauce

Ever since the first caveman put the first bronto-brisket on a fire, the barbecue arts have been dominated by the heavier sex. But more and more women are beginning to make their mark in the pit. Barbara Correll of Reston, Va., is one of them.

"I like to compete with men," Barbara says, and she isn't kidding. She used to race cars. Now she beats the boys on the barbecue circuit as chief cook for the Death Row team. She helped organize the 10-member crew because, well, she's from Texas and didn't much like the local barbecue she found when she and her husband, Stewart, moved to the Washington, D.C., area. That name — Death Row — refers to a skit they used to perform at cook-offs: Asked to choose his last meal, an inmate requests Barbara's brisket — "barbecue to die for."

We don't know about that, but we do know that this sauce took first place at the 1994 Jack Daniel's cook-off in Lynchburg, Tenn.

Makes about 3 1/2 cups

2 tablespoons vegetable oil
1/2 cup finely chopped onion
1 clove garlic, minced
2 cups ketchup
1/2 cup Jack Daniel's whiskey, divided
1/4 cup raspberry vinegar
1/4 cup Worcestershire sauce
3 tablespoons molasses
2 tablespoons yellow mustard
2 tablespoons soy sauce
2 tablespoons Crystal hot sauce (or 1 tablespoon Tabasco sauce)
1/2 teaspoon coarsely ground black pepper
1/4 teaspoon ground red pepper
1/4 teaspoon liquid smoke (optional)

- In a medium saucepan, heat oil over medium heat. Add onion and garlic, and sauté until tender, about 5 minutes.
- Add ketchup, 1/4 cup of the Jack Daniel's, raspberry vinegar, Worcestershire sauce, molasses, mustard, soy sauce, hot sauce and peppers. Mix thoroughly.
- Cook the mixture for 2 hours in the smoker or simmer over low heat 20 minutes on stove top, and add the liquid smoke. After cooking, stir in remaining 1/4 cup Jack Daniel's.
- Refrigerate unused sauce up to several weeks.

Uses: As a baste, finishing and table sauce on pork, beef and chicken. It's also good in baked beans.

TIM'S JAMAICAN RUM RUB

Makes about 1 1/2 cups

3/4 cup coarse kosher salt, or to taste
1/4 cup coarsely ground black pepper
1/4 cup vegetable oil
1/4 cup rum
1/4 cup Worcestershire sauce
3 tablespoons sugar
2 tablespoons red pepper flakes
1 tablespoon ground allspice
2 teaspoons fresh minced garlic
1 teaspoon powdered ginger

- In a small container, combine ingredients.
- Refrigerate unused sauce indefinitely.

Uses: As a rub for fresh ham, pork tenderloin or pork chops. Use judiciously — 1 tablespoon per pound of meat — because it's salty.

To use on ham: Have a butcher bone and butterfly an 8- to 10-pound fresh ham. Remove any loose fat, if desired, and score the meat side with a sharp knife.

- Lay ham skin side down. Rub about 1/3 of the mixture into the meat. Roll up ham, and wrap in aluminum foil; store in a sealed plastic bag in the refrigerator at least overnight or up to 2 days.
- In a covered grill over low heat, cook slowly in foil for 7 to 8 hours, or until meat thermometer registers 160 degrees.

Barbecue isn't an Olympic sport, but if it were, we have a gold medal candidate. Tim Patridge, program manager for catering with the Atlanta Committee for the Olympic Games, has loved barbecue since his boyhood on a farm outside Atlanta. His travels to places like Africa and the Caribbean have taught him about other barbecue styles. He united his experiences in this wet rub, which gets its kick from Jamaican rum.

GRILLED GARLIC WINE SAUCE

How can you possibly improve upon the flavor of a thick tenderloin steak grilled to medium-rare perfection? Surely not by smothering it with a thick glop of tomatoey barbecue sauce. We suggest a more subtle enhancement — like this sauce that helped win a National Beef Cook-off. The key ingredient is grilled or roasted garlic. When roasted, garlic softens to a buttery consistency, and its flavor turns from sharp and pungent to mellow and nutty. While you're at it, roast another garlic head to use as a spread for the crusty bread you'll likely be serving with your steak.

Makes about 1 cup

1 head garlic, unpeeled, separated into cloves
1 teaspoon olive oil
1 cup dry red wine
1/2 cup beef broth
4 tablespoons butter or margarine

- Place garlic cloves on a large piece of foil, and drizzle with oil. Wrap foil around garlic to enclose in several layers.
- Place on grid over medium-hot coals. Cook 20 to 30 minutes or until garlic is very soft, turning occasionally. (Alternatively, you can roast them in a 350-degree oven for about the same length of time.)
- Meanwhile, in a small saucepan, combine wine and beef broth, and bring to a simmer over low heat, either on the stove or grill top. Cook 10 to 15 minutes or until reduced to about 3/4 cup. Remove from heat.
- Remove garlic cloves from packet. Squeeze cloves to remove softened garlic from skins. Discard skins. Press peeled garlic through sieve into reserved wine mixture, and mix well. Stir in butter until blended. Serve warm.
- Refrigerate unused sauce up to several days.

Uses: As a table sauce for grilled tenderloin steaks. For extra flavor, rub the steaks before grilling with a mixture of cracked black peppercorns, coarse salt and crumbled bay leaf.

BRAVA TERRACE BARBECUE SAUCE

Makes about 2 quarts

1/4 cup peanut oil
3 medium onions, chopped
3 cloves garlic, minced
3 scotch bonnet or habañero peppers, seeded and
*   minced (wear rubber gloves)*
1 bay leaf
1 28-ounce can Italian plum tomatoes
2 12-ounce cans domestic beer
1 quart veal stock
1 cup packed brown sugar
3 tablespoons Worcestershire sauce
1 tablespoon ground cumin
1 1/2 tablespoons cornstarch
1/4 cup cold water

- In a large sauce pot, over medium-high heat sauté in oil the onion, garlic, peppers and bay leaf.
- When ingredients start to caramelize, add tomatoes (break up with wooden spoon), beer and stock.
- Reduce heat to medium. Cook about 30 minutes, or until the mixture is reduced by half.
- Add brown sugar, Worcestershire sauce and cumin.
- Mix cornstarch and water. Add this paste to sauce. Bring to a boil, and cook for 5 minutes. Serve warm.
- If you prefer a smooth sauce, purée in a blender or press through a sieve to strain.
- Refrigerate up to several days or freeze for longer storage.

Uses: As a finishing sauce for ribs, pork chops or chicken. Also a good base for chili.

The Napa Valley's Fred Halpert is one of those fortunate people whose expertise combines two culinary delights — barbecue and wine. Though the menu at Brava Terrace, his St. Helena, Calif., restaurant, reflects the techniques he learned working with three-star French chefs, he's also put to good use the grilling tricks he picked up at many a neighborhood cookout growing up in Miami. His grilled ribs and pork chops are customer favorites. It must be the sauce, which he developed for a "Ribs and Zin" cooking contest.

"It was a local competition with some winery guys. We all got ribs from Chicago and came up with our own sauces. I did one that used a veal stock base and scotch bonnet peppers. My ribs won, even though they never actually made it to the competition — they all got eaten up before it started."

His wine recommendation? "Zinfandels, definitely. They can handle the spices."

FRANCISCAN ZINFANDEL MARINADE

When we called the Napa Valley Vintners Association in the hopes of finding a good wine-based sauce, more than a dozen vineyards responded. We tried several recipes, but this full-flavored one from Franciscan Vineyards was our favorite.

Makes 1 quart

1 medium red onion, finely chopped
1 cup Franciscan Zinfandel or other dry red wine
2 cups chopped Pomi tomatoes (sold in cardboard containers in upscale supermarkets; canned chopped tomatoes may be substituted)
1/4 cup chili powder
1 teaspoon ground oregano
1/2 teaspoon ground cumin
1/2 teaspoon salt

- In a small glass or plastic bowl, soak onion in wine for 1 hour.
- In a medium glass or plastic bowl, mix the remaining ingredients into a smooth pulp with a wooden spoon.
- Blend onion-wine mixture into the tomato mixture.
- Refrigerate for at least 1 hour or up to 1 week, allowing flavors to blend.

Uses: As a table sauce for lamb, beef, chicken or pork. Place meat in marinade several hours or overnight before grilling. Leftover marinade may be heated, and served as a sauce on the side.

NATHALIE'S BARBECUE BREW

Makes about 6 cups

1/4 cup chili oil (found in Asian sections of most
supermarkets)
2 tablespoons chopped fresh ginger
1 large onion, chopped
5 cloves garlic, minced
1/4 cup chili powder
2 12-ounce cans beer (non-alcoholic beer is fine)
1 cup tomato juice or V-8 juice
1/2 cup Worcestershire sauce
Juice of 1 lemon or lime
5 tablespoons Dijon mustard
3 tablespoons paprika
2 tablespoons chopped fresh thyme, or 2 teaspoons dried
Salt and coarsely ground black pepper to taste

- In a saucepan, heat the oil over medium heat.
- Add ginger, onion, garlic and chili powder, and
  cook until soft.
- Add beer, tomato juice, Worcestershire sauce,
  lemon juice, mustard, paprika and thyme.
- Bring to a boil. Reduce heat to medium-low, and
  simmer for 5 to 10 minutes. Add salt and pepper.
  Let cool
- Refrigerate unused sauce up to several weeks.

Uses: As a marinade, baste and finishing sauce for
beef, pork or chicken.

To many Americans, beer is almost as much a part of barbecue as smoke and meat. Some cooks use it to marinate or mop. Most just use it to stoke their own internal fireboxes gulp by gulp. With all that brew flowing, you'd think more people would try it in their barbecue sauce.

Nathalie Dupree has tried it and come up with an unusual, contemporary taste. The renowned cooking show host and cookbook author has experimented with virtually every type of classic Southern barbecue sauce, but this one — adapted from her book *Matters of Taste* — has its roots in the Southwest. It's got bite.

CAFFÉ BARBECUE

Sounds like a trendy new grill on Melrose, doesn't it? It's our name for one of the oldest ideas in saucemaking. A cup of Joe gives tomato sauces an interesting undertone. This recipe, inspired by one in *Eating Well* magazine, called for strong coffee, so we went with one of the strongest: Starbucks dark Italian roast espresso. It's worth the lost sleep.

Makes about 2 cups

1 cup ketchup
3/4 cup brewed espresso (or other strong coffee)
1/4 cup molasses
2 tablespoons orange juice
2 tablespoons cider vinegar
2 teaspoons Worcestershire sauce
2 teaspoons Dijon mustard
2 jalapeño peppers, pierced all over with a fork
3 shots Tabasco sauce

- In a medium saucepan, combine all ingredients except Tabasco sauce. Cook, stirring, over low heat until slightly thickened, 10 to 15 minutes.
- Remove from heat, and let cool. Discard peppers. Season with Tabasco sauce.
- Refrigerate unused sauce up to several weeks.

Uses: On chicken, pork and beef. Biscotti optional.

Coca-Cola Barbecue Sauce

Makes about 3 cups

1 12-ounce can Coca-Cola Classic
1 1/2 cups ketchup
1 cup finely chopped onion
1/4 cup cider vinegar
1/4 cup Worcestershire sauce
1 teaspoon chili powder
1 teaspoon salt
Hot pepper sauce to taste

- In a medium saucepan, combine all ingredients. Bring to a boil. Reduce heat to medium-low, and simmer, covered, for 30 to 45 minutes or until sauce is thickened, stirring occasionally.
- Strain if desired. Season with hot pepper sauce.
- Refrigerate unused sauce up to several weeks.

Uses: As a finishing sauce for ribs, chicken and hamburgers.

In the South they take the Coca-Cola Co. literally when it says, "Things go better with Coke." Southerners use the soft drink in everything from cakes and puddings to baked beans and, yes, barbecue sauce. There have been countless Coca-Cola barbecue sauces over the years, some of them as simple as 1 part ketchup, 1 part Coke. We think you ought to go to a little more trouble than that. The recipe for this sauce comes from the archives at the company's home office in Atlanta. We've seen similar recipes using Pepsi, RC Cola and Dr Pepper. Just don't try diet drinks; the NutraSweet breaks down under heat.

JEANNE'S FLORIDA HORSERADISH SAUCE

It figures that horseradish, often eaten on seafood, would turn up in a Florida barbecue sauce. Food writer Jeanne Voltz was living there when she got this bold, sassy sauce from a lawyer friend in Jacksonville. "Back in the '50s, the golden age of charred meat and three-martini barbecues, we used to slather this stuff all over the place," she says. "I use it much more sparingly now, but it's still my favorite sauce."

Makes about 3 1/2 cups

1/2 cup (1 stick) butter or margarine
1 cup cider vinegar
1 cup ketchup
1 5- to 6-ounce jar horseradish
Juice of 6 lemons or limes
1 tablespoon Worcestershire sauce
1/2 teaspoon hot pepper sauce, or to taste
1/2 teaspoon salt, or to taste

- In a medium saucepan, melt butter over medium heat.
- Add remaining ingredients. Bring to a boil. Reduce heat to medium-low, and simmer, uncovered, for 20 to 25 minutes. Remove from heat and let cool.
- Refrigerate unused sauce up to several weeks.

Uses: As a basting and table sauce on pork and beef (using limes) and chicken and fish (using lemons). Don't overdo it with this sauce or your meat will taste like barbecued horseradish.

MEDITERRANEAN SUN-DRIED TOMATO MARINADE

Makes about 1 1/2 cups

5 cloves garlic, peeled
2 large shallots, peeled and quartered
1/2 cup dried tomatoes, soaked in warm water for 30
    minutes, and drained
2/3 cup olive oil
1/4 cup balsamic or red wine vinegar
2 tablespoons packed brown sugar
2 teaspoons red pepper flakes
2 teaspoons paprika
1 teaspoon ground cloves
1 teaspoon dried thyme
1 teaspoon salt
1/4 teaspoon ground red pepper

- In a food processor fitted with the steel blade and
  the motor running, drop garlic and shallots
  through the shoot to chop.
- When tomatoes are softened, drain, and add to the
  food processor bowl along with remaining
  ingredients. Process into a slightly chunky paste.
- Refrigerate unused sauce up to several weeks.

Uses: As a wet rub for pork or chicken. Cover 1 1/2
to 2 pounds of meat with the mixture, and chill for 2
hours or overnight. Stir the marinade after 1 hour.

We love what sun-dried tomatoes do to pasta sauce, so why not barbecue sauce? We coated chicken breasts with this intensely flavored paste, and our diners couldn't get enough. We credit the idea to cookbook author Jay Solomon, who recommends a similar sauce on pork loin or tenderloin, cubed and threaded on skewers.

SMOKE SIGNALS SAUCE

Here's what happens when a great American barbecue sauce collides with a great Tex-Mex salsa. We tried it at the urging of Park Kerr, proprietor of The El Paso Chile Company (see the final chapter for mail-order info) and author of *The El Paso Company's Texas Border Cookbook.* If you've never tried chipotle chilies — which are large jalapeños dried and smoked — head to your nearest Latin market (if your supermarket doesn't carry them) and stock several cans; their searing, smoky flavor is so tantalizing you'll want to toss them in everything.

Makes about 1 1/2 quarts

3 tablespoons olive oil
1 cup minced onion
3 cloves garlic, peeled and minced
1 tablespoon chili powder
1 28-ounce can crushed tomatoes with added purée
1 12-ounce bottle amber beer (such as Dos Equis)
1 cup tomato-based bottled hot salsa
1/2 cup ketchup
1/4 cup packed light brown sugar
4 canned chipotle chilies in adobo sauce, minced
3 tablespoons adobo sauce from the chipotle can
2 tablespoons cider vinegar
2 tablespoons unsulfured molasses
1/2 teaspoon liquid hickory smoke flavoring
1/2 teaspoon salt

- In a large saucepan, warm the olive oil over low heat. Add the onion and garlic, and cook, covered, stirring once or twice, 10 minutes.
- Stir in the chili powder and cook, covered, for 5 minutes.
- Stir in remaining ingredients. Cook, partially covered, stirring once or twice, until the sauce has thickened slightly and is shiny, about 30 minutes. Let cool.
- For smooth sauce, force it through a food mill or purée it in a food processor.
- Refrigerate unused sauce up to several weeks.

Uses: As a finishing sauce for ribs, chicken, burgers, brisket or shrimp. Also a good base for chili.

LEMON-THYME BARBECUE SAUCE

Makes 3/4 cup

3 tablespoons white wine vinegar
1 tablespoon lemon juice
2 teaspoons Dijon mustard
1 shallot, minced
5 or 6 green onions, white part only, chopped
2 tablespoons chopped fresh lemon thyme (or 2
 tablespoons regular thyme, plus 1 teaspoon grated
 lemon peel)
1/4 cup minced fresh parsley
3 tablespoons vegetable oil
3 tablespoons olive oil
Salt and pepper to taste

- In a medium glass bowl, combine all ingredients. Let sit 30 minutes before using.
- Best used the day you make it, but will keep, refrigerated, a few days.

Uses: As a marinade or table sauce for grilled seafood, chicken, or vegetables. Also good over boiled potatoes. Or, double the recipe and use as both a marinade and table sauce.

Not many traditional barbecue sauces would pair well with delicate fish, but this is hardly a traditional barbecue sauce. It's adapted from one we spotted in a most unlikely place: a catalog for Shepherd's Garden Seeds. They offered it as a suggestion for getting some culinary mileage out of the lemon thyme plants they sell. But since our herb garden was fresh out, we used regular thyme with a little lemon zest thrown in.

LOUISIANA BACON-PECAN BARBECUE SAUCE

Watch out: This sauce, inspired by Cajun-cooking king Paul Prudhomme, can be so addictive, you may not have enough left to baste your meat with by the time you're ready to grill. One taster said she would be perfectly content to eat it as is, with a spoon. But trust us — it's even better as a smoky-sweet, slightly crunchy glaze.

Makes about 1 quart

8 ounces sliced bacon
1 1/2 cups sliced onions
4 cloves garlic, sliced
1 12-ounce bottle chili sauce
1 14 1/2-ounce can beef broth
1 cup honey
3/4 cup coarsely chopped roasted pecans
Juice from 1 orange
Rind from 1/2 orange, quartered
Juice from 1 lemon
Rind from 1/2 lemon, quartered
1 teaspoon black pepper
1 teaspoon white pepper
1/2 teaspoon ground red pepper
Tabasco sauce to taste
2 tablespoons unsalted butter

- In a large saucepan over medium-high heat, fry the bacon until crisp.
- Remove bacon to paper towels to drain; pour off all but 3 tablespoons bacon grease.
- Reduce heat to medium. Stir onions and garlic into the bacon grease and sauté until golden and tender. Add chili sauce, broth, honey, pecans, cooked bacon, juice and rinds from oranges and lemons, and peppers.
- Bring to a boil, reduce heat to low and simmer about 15 minutes, stirring occasionally.
- Pour mixture into blender or food processor fitted with a steel blade and process until bacon and

pecans are finely chopped.

- Return mixture to the saucepan. Stir in butter and heat just until melted; season to taste with Tabasco.
- Refrigerate up to a several days; freeze for longer storage.

Uses: As a baste and table sauce for all kinds of pork — especially ribs, tenderloins and pork roasts. For something different, use to baste kebabs of pork, parboiled sweet potato chunks and pineapple cubes before grilling.

Don't forget the buns: Barbecue used to be street slang for a good-looking woman, which is why Louis Armstrong recorded a 1927 song called "Struttin' With Some Barbecue."

Maple-Juniper Marinade and Glaze

Pungent, purplish juniper berries, an essential flavoring for gin, are typically paired with venison, pâtés, sausages and other strong-flavored meats. But Jody Adams, chef at Rialto in Cambridge, Mass., had another idea: Combine the berries with garlic, bay leaves and other potent herbs along with maple syrup to make a marinade for pork chops. We tried it and loved it, and we aren't the only ones. Her novel recipe was a finalist in the National Pork Producers Council's Lick Your Chops contest. You may have to go to a gourmet market for juniper berries, but they're worth the search.

Marinade

Makes about 2/3 cup

1/4 cup maple syrup
3 tablespoons olive oil
2 tablespoons balsamic vinegar
2 shallots, thinly sliced
4 bay leaves, finely chopped
2 tablespoons coarsely chopped juniper berries
1 tablespoon chopped fresh sage (or 1 teaspoon dried)
2 teaspoons minced garlic
1 teaspoon cracked black peppercorns

Finishing glaze

Makes 1/4 cup

2 tablespoons maple syrup
1 tablespoon olive oil
1 tablespoon balsamic vinegar

- In a small bowl, combine marinade ingredients.
- In another small bowl, combine glaze ingredients.
- Refrigerate unused sauce 1 week, unused marinade indefinitely.

Uses: As a marinade and finishing sauce for chicken, quail or all kinds of pork. This is the recipe that captured the taste buds of the pork producers:

Maple-Juniper Glazed Pork Chops

- In a shallow baking dish, pour marinade, and place 6 1 1/4-inch-thick pork chops. Turn to coat. Cover and refrigerate 6 hours or overnight.
- Drain chops, discarding marinade. Sprinkle with salt to taste.
- Place chops on a kettle-style grill directly over medium-hot coals, lower grill hood, and grill for 12 to 16 minutes, turning once, until chops are barely done.
- Brush chops with syrup mixture. Lower hood, and grill for 1 minute longer.

A recipe we passed up: In the movie *Fried Green Tomatoes*, everyone loves the Whistle Stop Cafe's barbecue. But when she's complimented for it, the cook just smiles and chirps, "The secret's in the sauce." The secret ingredient? Good ole boy au jus.

KOSHER CAJUN BARBECUE SAUCE AND RUB

When it comes to barbecue cook-offs, kosher Jews tend to get left out in the cold. But who says you have to invite a pig to such an event? Certainly not the organizers of the annual Solomon Schechter Day School Kosher Rib Burn-off in Cleveland. They invited barbecue fans to enter their best beef ribs in a competition that became an annual event. This recipe comes from Cindy Keller and her sister, Ellen Wohl, who won first place in the 1994 contest. The main ingredient: a commercial sauce bearing, of course, the kosher seal.

SAUCE

Makes 1 cup

1/2 cup prepared barbecue sauce (they use Kraft Thick and Spicy)
1/2 cup honey
1 1/2 teaspoons Cajun seasoning for meat
3/4 teaspoon paprika

RUB

Makes 2 tablespoons

2 teaspoons salt
2 teaspoons garlic powder
1 teaspoon Cajun seasoning
1 teaspoon coarsely ground black pepper

- In a small bowl, combine sauce ingredients.
- In a small bowl, combine rub ingredients.

Uses: As a rub and marinating/finishing sauce for 6 pounds of beef flanken or short ribs.

KOSHER-CAJUN RIBS

- Clean ribs. Sprinkle with rub mixture.
- Place in a baking pan in a single layer, add a little water, cover, and steam ribs in a 350-degree oven for 1 hour.
- Pour sauce over ribs, and refrigerate overnight.
- Finish off on the grill, basting with the sauce.

GILROY GARLIC BARBECUE DRESSING

Makes about 3 cups

2 cups hot water
2/3 cup distilled vinegar
1/2 cup vegetable or olive oil
15 whole black peppercorns
10 cloves garlic, crushed
4 bay leaves, crushed
2 to 3 tablespoons minced fresh parsley (or 1 tablespoon dried)
1 1/2 tablespoons dried oregano
1 tablespoon salt
1 teaspoon dried rosemary

- Combine ingredients in jar with tight-fitting lid, and shake well.
- Refrigerate overnight or longer — the longer the stinkier. Sauce will keep, refrigerated, indefinitely.

Uses: As a basting sauce or marinade for any kind of grilled meat, chicken, fish or even vegetables. Baste meat several times while cooking.

Will Rogers once described Gilroy, Calif., ("The Garlic Capital of the World") as "the only town in America where you can marinate a steak just by hanging it out on a clothesline." We can't top that. Here's a classic recipe from the Gilroy Garlic Festival's *Garlic Lover's Cookbook*. It's the sauce that keeps on giving.

INTERNATIONAL FLAVORS

Americans sometimes talk like they're the only people on Earth who know barbecue. They're not, of course. The very word barbecue testifies to far-flung roots; it comes from *barbacoa,* the term Spanish explorers used to describe the framework of branches they found Caribbean natives using to smoke meat.

Jeanne Voltz, author of *Barbecued Ribs, Smoked Butts and Other Great Feeds,* has researched this question of origins. "As far as I can tell, barbecue came to this country through Florida with DeSoto, who got it from the Caribbeans, who probably got it from the Africans. And the native Americans were already doing something like it."

A great smoke ring of cultures around the globe was grilling and barbecuing before the first Carolinian picked the first pig. Malaysia's satay, Japan's yakitori, Jamaica's jerk   each name summons different customs, perhaps different meats, certainly different flavors.

For her part, Jeanne Voltz says that some of the best barbecue she ever ate was a haunch of Brazilian beef basted in peppered vinegar and dipped in manioc meal. "The gauchos take barbecue very seriously," she says.

That's quite a compliment coming from someone raised on Alabama pork.

UPPER MISSISSIPPI JERK PASTE

What's a nice jerk like this doing in a place like Minnesota?

Since the 1700s, Jamaicans have been grilling pork and chicken in jerk rubs and pastes, a festival of Caribbean peppers and seasonings that induces sweet-spicy flashes. It's an indication of how popular jerk has become that you find cooks all over the hemisphere playing with it. Though she lives thousands of miles from Kingston, Minneapolis chef Lissa Michalsky has studied Jamaican cooking for years. She and her husband, Pat Kinney, run the Upper Mississippi Sauce Co., whose traditional tomato-based barbecue sauce won first place at the 1994 American Royal contest. She created this jerk paste and uses it with a pork recipe that combines the best of the Caribbean and the best of all-American barbecue.

Makes about 2 1/2 cups

1/2 cup vegetable oil
1/4 cup cider vinegar
1 large red onion, minced
9 green onions, minced
4 to 6 habañero peppers, minced (or, if you must, 8 jalapeños)
1/4 cup chopped fresh thyme (or 2 tablespoons dried)
3 tablespoons minced ginger (or 1 tablespoon powdered)
1 tablespoon minced garlic (or 1 teaspoon powdered)
1 tablespoon ground black pepper
1 tablespoon salt
1 tablespoon allspice
2 teaspoons nutmeg
2 teaspoons cinnamon

- In a small bowl, combine oil, vinegar, onions, peppers, thyme (not dry), ginger (not powdered) and garlic (not powdered).
- In a separate bowl, combine black pepper, salt, allspice, nutmeg, cinnamon and dried substitutes for thyme, ginger and garlic (if used).
- Combine the two mixtures.
- Marinade is best if used immediately but will keep several days in refrigerator.

Uses: On chicken or pork, such as:

Upper Mississippi Jerk Pork

- Trim fat from a 5- to 6-pound pork shoulder or butt.
- Cut large slits in top and sides of roast to score fat and create pouches for the jerk mixture.
- Wearing gloves, slather meat inside and out, stuffing pouches.
- Place in a gallon Ziploc bag, seal, and refrigerate overnight — preferably longer.
- To smoke or roast in the oven, follow pork shoulder instructions in the introductory chapter. If desired, baste with Upper Mississippi barbecue sauce or other tomato-based barbecue sauce during last hour, and serve additional sauce on the side. For information on Upper Mississippi sauce, see final chapter.

Don't slop it on your shirt: Monte Carlo's Louis XV restaurant serves a $60 dish of barbecued scallops finished with a few drops of Balsamic Traditional vinegar. At $150 for a tenth of a liter, it may be the world's most expensive barbecue sauce.

OAXACAN RED CHILE BARBECUE SAUCE

In the Mexican state of Oaxaca, this pleasantly hot sauce would most likely be spread on *barbacoa* roasts that have been steamed in a rock oven underground. They do it a little differently at Zarela, a Manhattan restaurant that lures flocks of foodies with its contemporary Mexican cuisine. This sauce was inspired by chef-owner Zarela Martinez's book *Food From My Heart*. Though intended for pork ribs, we thought it was terrific on grilled shrimp, too.

Makes about 2 cups

3 to 4 ounces dried ancho, guajillo, New Mexico or dried (not canned) chipotle chilies, tops removed and seeded (see note)
10 large cloves garlic, peeled
2 tablespoons red wine vinegar
2 teaspoons dried Mexican oregano
1/2 cup honey, or to taste
1/4 to 1/2 cup yellow mustard, or to taste
Salt and freshly ground black pepper to taste

- Cover chilies with boiling water, and soak until softened, about 10 minutes. Drain chilies, and discard all but 1/2 cup of the liquid.
- Place chilies, reserved liquid and garlic in a blender. Process 1 minute, and scrape down the sides with a rubber spatula.
- Add vinegar and oregano. Process again until smooth.
- With a wooden spoon, press the purée through a sieve into a bowl, discarding solids.
- Whisk in the honey and mustard. Season with salt and pepper.
- Refrigerate unused sauce up to 2 weeks.

Uses: As a finishing and table sauce on ribs, chicken and seafood.

Note: Zarela says the original recipe used hard-to-find smoked Oaxacan pasilla chilies; we tried it with the New Mexico chilies readily available at our neighborhood supermarket, with excellent results.

CUBAN MOJO CRIOLLO

Makes 1 1/2 cups

6 large cloves garlic, minced
1 teaspoon ground cumin
1/2 teaspoon salt
1/2 teaspoon dried oregano
3/4 cup orange juice
1/4 cup lime juice
1/2 cup olive oil (preferably Spanish)
Coarsely ground black pepper to taste

- Using a fork, mash garlic to a paste with cumin, salt and oregano. (This can be done with a mortar and pestle.)
- In a small bowl, place the mixture and add orange and lime juices.
- Meanwhile, in a saucepan, heat the oil until hot, but not boiling.
- Remove oil from the heat, and whisk in the garlic-juice mixture. Season with pepper.
- Sauce is best if used immediately but will keep several days in refrigerator.

Uses: As a finishing sauce for grilled seafood, chicken and meats, as well as boiled vegetables.

This tart, garlicky sauce — sort of a cooked vinaigrette — is a staple in Cuban kitchens and is widely available in Latin markets and some supermarkets. It's sprinkled on grilled foods as well as Cuban sandwiches, boiled yuca and other tubers. The most authentic versions use the juice of the bumpy, green sour orange; if you can't find them do as we did: use a combination of orange and lime juice.

MEXICAN MOLE BARBECUE SAUCE AND MARINADE

Oaxaca has been called "the land of the seven moles," but this recipe isn't one of them. Moles — complex sauces thickened with ground nuts, seeds and dried chilies — enrich all kinds of roasted, braised and fricasseed meats in Mexico, as well as enchiladas. Mary Ann Clayton, who styled the photos for this book, undertook an intensive study of moles during a stay in Oaxaca several years ago. OK, she pigged out. She helped us concoct this simpler mole for grilled meats. It's dark, rich and delectable enough to eat with a spoon — largely because of an ingredient common to classic moles: bittersweet chocolate.

Makes about 4 cups

4 dried ancho or New Mexico chili peppers, stemmed and seeded
2 cups water
2 canned chipotle chilies in adobo sauce
2 tablespoons canola or vegetable oil
2 large fresh Anaheim peppers, stemmed, seeded and chopped
1 cup chopped onion
1 tablespoon minced garlic
1/3 cup raw peanuts
1 tablespoon sesame seeds
1 10 3/4-ounce can tomato purée
2 tablespoons peanut butter
1 tablespoon allspice
1 tablespoon cinnamon
2 teaspoons adobo seasoning (available in Latin markets and many supermarkets)
2 ounces grated bittersweet chocolate (or 1 ounce each semisweet and unsweetened chocolate)

- On a hot griddle, roast prepared ancho peppers until limp. Do not burn.
- Transfer anchos to a heavy saucepan, and add water. Bring to a boil. Remove from heat. Add chipotle peppers, including the sauce that clings to them, and let stand.
- Place oil in a skillet over medium-low heat. When hot, add Anaheim peppers, onion, garlic, peanuts and sesame seeds. Sauté until onions are translucent, about 10 minutes.

- Drain ancho and chipotle, reserving liquid.
- In a blender or food processor fitted with a steel blade, combine the ancho and chipotles with sautéed mixture, tomato purée, peanut butter, allspice, cinnamon, adobo seasoning and 1 cup of the reserved ancho and chipotle liquid; process until smooth.
- Return mixture to saucepan. Bring to a boil. Reduce heat to low, add chocolate, and continue to stir until chocolate is melted. Cover and simmer 20 minutes, stirring occasionally, adding reserved ancho water as needed. Add more adobo seasoning if needed.
- Refrigerate unused sauce up to 2 weeks.

MARINADE

1/2 cup lime juice
1 tablespoon canola oil

- Transfer 1/2 cup of mole to a glass bowl. Add lime juice and oil.

Uses: As a marinade and finishing sauce for turkey, chicken or pork. Cover up to 2 pounds of meat with marinade at least 1 hour before grilling. Serve with mole sauce.

Texas takeout: In John Wayne's movie The Alamo, Davy and the boys get sick on salt pork and decide to make a daring raid behind Mexican lines to rustle some cattle. Afterwards, digging into beef ribs, one of the buckskins says what Texans have been saying ever since: "Hog never could rightly pass for meat — but beef ..."

Gaucho Green Sauce (Chimichuri)

In Argentine steakhouses, chimichuri — a spiced parsley sauce that's like a vinegary pesto — is as much a table fixture as ketchup in American burger joints. But when we put it out in a bowl at a backyard barbecue, one guest couldn't get over the color. We'll spare you his comments about what it was as green as. Suffice to say that once he tasted it, he went back for more.

Makes 1 1/2 cups

1 bunch parsley, stemmed and coarsely chopped (about 2 packed cups)
6 to 8 cloves garlic, minced
3/4 cup olive oil
1/4 cup red wine vinegar
2 tablespoons lemon juice
1/2 teaspoon salt, or to taste
1/2 teaspoon ground black pepper, or to taste
1/4 teaspoon ground red pepper, or to taste

• In a blender or food processor fitted with steel blade, combine ingredients. Process about 10 seconds.
• Sauce is best if used immediately but will keep several days in refrigerator.

Uses: On grilled meats (especially steak), chicken, seafood, even vegetables. If you like, dip warm flour tortillas into the sauce.

PAPA VITO'S AMMOGGHIO

Makes about 2 1/2 cups

8 to 10 cloves garlic, peeled and chopped
2 teaspoons salt
1 teaspoon dried oregano
1/2 teaspoon coarsely ground black pepper
3 or 4 fresh, peeled Italian plum tomatoes (or drained, peeled, canned tomatoes if fresh are out of season), chopped
1/4 cup chopped fresh basil leaves
1/2 to 1 cup water
1/2 cup Italian extra-virgin olive oil (Vito prefers Merro brand)

* In a wooden mortar or bowl, place the garlic and salt. Mash to a paste with pestle or fork.
* Add oregano, pepper and tomatoes, and mash. Stir in basil leaves, 1/2 cup of water and oil. If it's too thick or too strong for your taste (Vito likes it garlicky), add more water.
* Sauce is best if used immediately but will keep several days in refrigerator.

Uses: As a marinade, baste and table sauce for grilled chicken or fish (such as swordfish, mackerel or striped bass). Also good over sliced, grilled eggplant and grilled bread. And, yes, it makes a good pasta sauce. Vito suggests serving it with slices of Pecorino cheese on the side.

Susan first tasted this Old World sauce at the New World home of her sister's father-in-law. When Papa Vito grills at his Staten Island house, he uses ammogghio sauce ("a mish-mash," he says) from his native Sicily. "In the summertime, I would say maybe 95 percent of the cooking there is done outside. Most of us have a charcoal grill and a big copper pot for cooking our pasta on a wood stove. Even our pasta has a better taste because it's cooked over wood." (Naturally, pasta is the traditional opening course at a Sicilian cookout.)

When Susan visited, Vito was about to toss some chicken on the grill. He explained the sauce at the dining room table, then moved to the kitchen counter. "I show you," he said. With a wooden mortar and pestle, he deftly mashed the ingredients together. "Here, you try it," he offered, setting a bowl of sauce on the table with Italian bread for dipping. Soon he was mixing another batch because Susan and the others got so carried away they didn't leave much for the chicken.

"It's nothing special," the modest Vito said of his sauce. "Everybody in Sicily makes this."

ETHIOPIAN PEPPERY SPICE PASTE (BERBERÉ)

Massachusetts is not exactly a mecca for great barbecue, and most of what's there is imported — from the South or some other part of the world. At the East Coast Grill and Jake and Earl's take-out in Cambridge, chef Chris Schlesinger's imaginative menus draw from his Virginia upbringing and his travels to pepper-loving countries. Chris, a prolific cookbook author, smears a fire-breathing Ethiopian paste like this one on chicken legs, then pops them in the fridge to marinate a couple of hours before grilling. Accompaniments? Fresh lemon wedges for squeezing over the hot drumsticks — and ice-cold beer.

Makes about 1 1/2 cups

1/2 cup paprika
2 tablespoons ground red pepper
2 tablespoons salt
1 tablespoon cracked black pepper
1 tablespoon red pepper flakes
1 tablespoon five-spice powder
1 tablespoon dry mustard
2 teaspoons ground coriander
1 teaspoon powdered ginger
1 teaspoon ground cardamom
1 teaspoon turmeric
1 teaspoon cinnamon
1 teaspoon allspice
1 teaspoon crushed fenugreek seeds (optional)
1/2 teaspoon nutmeg
1/2 cup dry red wine
1/4 cup peanut oil
1/4 cup orange juice

- In a bowl, combine all ingredients through nutmeg.
- In a skillet, warm spices over medium heat, stirring, until very fragrant (2 to 3 minutes).
- Add red wine to the spice mixture, and cook 2 to 3 minutes, stirring constantly, to form a paste.
- Remove paste from heat, and let cool.
- Add oil and orange juice.
- Refrigerate unused paste up to a week. Bring to room temperature before using.

Uses: As a wet rub for chicken, pork or beef. (Chris recommends drumsticks; this makes enough to cover 16).

Secret Asian Sauce

Makes about 2 cups

5 cloves garlic, minced
1/2 cup hoisin sauce
1/4 cup plum sauce
1/4 cup minced green onion
1/4 cup minced cilantro leaves
3 tablespoons oyster sauce
2 tablespoons minced fresh ginger
2 tablespoons red wine vinegar
2 tablespoons honey
1 1/2 tablespoons roasted sesame seeds
1 tablespoon soy sauce
1 tablespoon dry sherry
2 teaspoons dark sesame oil
1 1/2 teaspoons grated lemon zest
1 1/2 teaspoons grated orange zest
1 1/2 teaspoons Asian chili sauce
1 teaspoon curry powder (optional)
1/4 teaspoon five-spice powder (optional)

- In a large bowl, combine all ingredients.
  Marinade will keep for several days in refrigerator
  (indefinitely, if you omit the green onion and
  cilantro).

Uses: As a baste and finishing sauce for ribs; as a
marinade for lamb, pork chops or chicken; as a glaze
for sea bass or other fish.

San Francisco chef Hugh
Carpenter has made a career
of mixing and matching Eastern
and Western ingredients and
techniques. We especially like
this clever combination of mostly
Asian pantry staples, adapted
from his *Fusion Food Cookbook*.

APRICOT BRAAI

Braai means barbecue and *vleis* means meat in the Afrikaans language of South Africa. "We're avid barbecuers," says Paul Zway, a South African grillmaster, and we believe him. A South African friend told us that the commercial jingle Americans remember as "baseball, hot dogs, apple pie and Chevrolet" had a different lyric in Johannesburg: "braaivleis, rugby, sunny skies and Chevrolet." Now living in Tucson, Ariz., Paul is marketing his trans-Atlantic barbecue expertise through a line of equipment and spices called Braai-B-Q Products. Here's a sauce he created that'll take half the contents of your pantry. It may sound odd, but it works.

Makes about 5 cups

1 cup smooth apricot jam
1 cup ketchup
3/4 cup herb vinegar
3/4 cup olive oil
1/4 cup yellow mustard
1 large onion, finely chopped
10 lemon leaves, finely chopped (optional)
8 cloves garlic, finely chopped
2 tablespoons Worcestershire sauce
1 tablespoon coffee granules
1 tablespoon turmeric
1 tablespoon fines herbes (mixed dry herbs)
2 teaspoons paprika
1 teaspoon curry powder
1 teaspoon salt
1 teaspoon coarsely ground black pepper
Chili powder to taste

- In a large plastic container, combine ingredients.
- Refrigerate unused sauce up to 2 weeks.

Uses: Add beef, pork or chicken to the sauce. Let marinate for about 6 hours, turning occasionally. Remove meat from marinade, and grill. Meanwhile, bring remaining sauce to boil. Reduce heat to medium-low and simmer for 5 minutes. Serve hot as a condiment for meat and vegetables.

Moroccan-Spiced Yogurt Marinade

Makes 1 1/2 cups

3/4 cup plain yogurt
1/3 cup lime juice
1/4 cup chopped parsley
1/4 cup chopped cilantro
2 tablespoons olive oil
2 tablespoons honey
1/2 teaspoon turmeric
1/4 teaspoon cardamom
1/4 teaspoon cinnamon
1/4 teaspoon allspice
1/4 teaspoon cumin
1/4 teaspoon salt
1/4 teaspoon ground red pepper
1/4 teaspoon ground black pepper
Hot pepper sauce to taste

- In a small bowl, combine all ingredients.
- Marinade is best if used immediately but will keep up to 1 week in refrigerator.

Uses: As a marinade and baste for fish, shrimp, chicken or lamb. Chicken or lamb may be cubed and kebabed on skewers with chunks of zucchini and red or yellow bell pepper. Coat all sides of meat with sauce, and marinate for 2 to 12 hours. Grill meat, brushing with marinade during the last 10 to 15 minutes of cooking.

Americans eat tons of yogurt, but they don't often think of cooking with it. Other cultures are well aware of its flavoring and tenderizing abilities. In India yogurt is used in tandoori cooking, their version of barbecue. In the Middle East it's used to marinate a variety of meats before grilling. The flavors of this particular marinade lean toward Morocco — especially if couscous, the grainlike North African pasta now available in most supermarkets, is served as an accompaniment.

MIDDLE EASTERN POMEGRANATE-MINT MARINADE

Kristin Eddy, a food-writing colleague of ours at the newspaper, has some interesting things in her kitchen — rose water, ground sumac, pomegranate syrup. They may seem a bit exotic to us, but they're perfectly natural to Kristin. As the child of a foreign service officer stationed in the Middle East, she always associated barbecue with her mother's grilled lamb kebabs. The inspiration for this aromatic marinade and baste comes from Kristin's birthplace in Lebanon and her childhood in Turkey. Pomegranates are also prized in the ancient cuisines of Persia and western Asia. Don't worry: You don't have to squeeze all those tiny crimson seeds. Middle Eastern markets here carry pomegranate syrup, the dark, concentrated juice of unsweetened pomegranates — as much a pantry staple in that part of the world as soy sauce is in the Far East.

Makes 3/4 cup

1/2 cup grated onion
1/4 cup beef or lamb broth
2 tablespoons pomegranate syrup or concentrate
1 tablespoon olive oil
1 tablespoon dried mint
1 teaspoon salt
1/2 teaspoon coarsely ground black pepper

- In a large bowl, combine ingredients.
- Marinade is best if used immediately but will keep up to several days in refrigerator.

Uses: As a marinade for lamb, beef or pork. (If pork, substitute chicken broth.)

For kebabs: Cube up to 2 pounds of meat, and toss with marinade. Cover, and refrigerate at least 4 hours, turning meat occasionally. Thread on skewers (with onion, tomato and green pepper if desired), and grill or broil. Offer small bowls of pomegranate syrup for dipping after grilling.

TURKISH MARINADE WITH CUMIN AND HERBS

Makes about 1 1/2 cups

1 medium onion, thinly sliced
1/3 cup olive oil
Juice of 1 lemon
1/3 cup minced fresh parsley leaves
1/3 cup minced fresh mint leaves
1 tablespoon minced fresh thyme leaves
3 large cloves garlic, minced
1 tablespoon paprika
2 teaspoons ground cumin
1/2 teaspoon red pepper flakes
Salt and coarsely ground black pepper to taste

- In a glass or plastic container large enough to hold meat, combine ingredients.
- Marinade is best if used immediately but will keep up to a few days in refrigerator.

Uses: As a marinade for up to 2 pounds of lamb, chicken, shrimp or scallops. For kebabs, see preceding recipe.

Something about shish kebabs summons images of Ward Cleaver giving June a break from the meatloaf grind. Back in the '50s, skewered beef and veggies were the height of cookout chic. But Ward probably never thought to season them with anything more adventurous than salt, pepper and MSG. We've got an idea, Ward — wherever you are. It probably originated in some Turkish kebab shop, where they flavor skewered meats with herb-redolent marinades. We adapted this recipe from one in Ayla Algar's *Classical Turkish Cooking*. Even the Beave would've liked it.

Curried Chutney Marinade and Dipping Sauce

This recipe originated not in India but in the test kitchens of the National Livestock and Meat Board in Chicago as an exotic way to jazz up beef strips. It wouldn't be in their best interest to tell you that the sauce works well with chicken or pork — so we will.

Marinade

Makes about 1/2 cup

1/4 cup Major Grey mango chutney, finely chopped
2 tablespoons cider vinegar
2 tablespoons water
1 teaspoon curry powder
1/8 teaspoon ground red pepper

Dipping Sauce

Makes about 3/4 cup

1/2 cup plain yogurt
3 tablespoons Major Grey's mango chutney, finely chopped
1 teaspoon lemon juice
1/2 teaspoon curry powder
1/8 teaspoon ground cumin
1/8 teaspoon ground red pepper

- In a plastic bag or container, combine marinade ingredients.
- In a small bowl, combine dipping sauce ingredients. Cover, and refrigerate. Remove 10 minutes before serving.
- Marinade and dipping sauce will keep up to 1 week in refrigerator.

Use in Curried Beef Kebabs

- Partially freeze (about 30 minutes) 1 pound of 1-inch-thick boneless beef top round, flank or sirloin steak. Trim excess fat. Cut meat into 1/8- to 1/4-inch-thick strips.
- Place in marinade, turning to coat. Marinate in refrigerator 6 hours, turning occasionally. Discard marinade.
- Thread beef on bamboo skewers that have been soaked in cold water for at least 30 minutes. Grill over medium coals 3 to 5 minutes, turning once. Serve with Dipping Sauce.

Barbecutie: Not long after Barbie debuted in 1959, Mattel introduced one of the first specialty models — Barbecue Barbie, with a cookout ensemble that included an apron and itty-bitty grilling utensils.

Satay Peanut Sauce

Did we tell you about the time Susan almost screwed up the satay? She was new in town and wanted to impress her co-workers with a dinner party showing off her knowledge of international cuisine. She chose satays, the skewered snacks Malaysians have sold on street corners for centuries. Three kinds of meat were marinating. The peanut sauce turned out perfect. Just one problem: She forgot the tiny bamboo skewers. Her guests ended up spearing the little morsels with toothpicks. They must not have minded — nearly everyone wanted the recipe.

Makes about 2 1/2 cups

1/4 cup peanut oil
1 cup chopped onion
1/4 cup minced fresh ginger
3 tablespoons minced garlic
1 teaspoon red pepper flakes
1 cup chunky or smooth peanut butter
3 tablespoons sugar
3/4 to 1 1/2 cups canned unsweetened coconut milk
1/3 cup soy sauce
3 tablespoons lime juice
1/4 cup chopped cilantro leaves

- In large skillet, place oil over medium heat. Add onion, ginger, garlic and red pepper flakes, and sauté until onions are tender, about 10 minutes.
- Stir in peanut butter, sugar, 3/4 cup of the coconut milk, soy sauce and lime juice. Cook 5 minutes longer, stirring frequently.
- Remove pan from heat. Stir in cilantro, and serve warm or at room temperature. If too thick, thin with coconut milk or water.
- Refrigerate unused sauce up to 1 week.

Uses: As a dipping sauce for chicken, beef (sirloin or flank steak) or lamb cubed or cut into thin strips. Thread on small bamboo skewers that have soaked in cold water at least 30 minutes. Shrimp or chicken livers would also work well.

Let 1 to 1 1/2 pounds of meat soak first for at least 30 minutes or overnight in one of the following marinades. Then grill or broil. Serve with saffron rice and peanut sauce for dipping.

SATAY MARINADE FOR CHICKEN OR SHRIMP

Makes about 1/2 cup

1/4 cup soy sauce
2 tablespoons sugar
1 tablespoon rice wine vinegar
1 tablespoon peanut oil
2 teaspoons minced garlic
1 teaspoon ground coriander
1 teaspoon powdered ginger

• In a large bowl, combine ingredients.

SATAY MARINADE FOR BEEF, LAMB OR CHICKEN LIVERS

Makes about 1/2 cup

1/4 cup sliced onion
2 cloves garlic, peeled and sliced
1 tablespoon molasses
1 tablespoon soy sauce
1 tablespoon peanut oil
1 tablespoon sugar
2 teaspoons lime juice
1 teaspoon ground cumin

• In a blender or food processor, combine ingredients.

Sauce Cities USA: According to Information Resources, the highest per capita consumption of barbecue sauce can be found in St. Louis, Memphis, Louisville and Little Rock. The lowest is in San Diego, Buffalo, Green Bay and New York City.

VIETNAMESE LEMON GRASS WET RUB

Lemon grass would certainly qualify as one of the fashionable ingredients of the '90s. With the growing popularity of Thai and Vietnamese cuisines, trend-conscious American chefs are finding ways to incorporate the fragrant, lemony tropical grass into their menus. It's the magic ingredient in this marinade for skewered beef or chicken strips, adapted from Nicole Routhier's *The Foods of Vietnam*. Serve as is or with a dipping sauce (Bangkok Dipping Sauce on page 105 or Satay Peanut Sauce on page 102 would work). If you really want to get authentic, remove the meat from skewers and wrap it in lettuce leaves with sprouts, cucumber slices, fresh cilantro and mint.

Makes about 3/4 cup

*2 stalks fresh lemon grass, outer leaves and upper half
  discarded, minced*
2 large shallots, peeled and sliced
5 cloves garlic, crushed
1 tablespoon sugar
2 teaspoons red pepper flakes
2 tablespoons nuoc mam (Vietnamese fish sauce)
1 tablespoon Oriental sesame oil
1 tablespoon peanut oil
2 tablespoons sesame seed (optional)

- In a spice grinder or small food processor, combine lemon grass, shallots, garlic, sugar and red pepper flakes, and process as finely as possible. (Or pound to a paste with mortar and pestle.)
- Transfer paste to a large bowl. Stir in fish sauce, sesame oil, peanut oil and sesame seed, if using.
- Marinade is best if used immediately but will keep up to 1 week in refrigerator.

Uses: As a marinade for 1 to 1 1/2 pounds of very thin strips of sirloin or rump roast, or chicken tenders. Coat with rub and let marinate for 30 minutes. Weave on bamboo skewers (soaked in cold water), then grill.

BANGKOK BARBECUE MARINADE AND DIPPING SAUCE

MARINADE

Makes 1 1/2 cups

1 cup coconut milk
3 tablespoons fish sauce
2 tablespoons chopped garlic
2 tablespoons chopped cilantro roots or stems
1 1/2 teaspoons ground black pepper
1 teaspoon ground turmeric
1 teaspoon curry powder

DIPPING SAUCE

Makes 3/4 cup

1/2 cup distilled vinegar
1/2 cup water
1/2 cup sugar
1 tablespoon minced garlic
2 teaspoons sambal oelek (Asian chili sauce)
1/2 teaspoon salt

- In a glass or plastic container large enough to hold meat, combine marinade ingredients.
- In a small saucepan, combine dipping sauce ingredients. Bring to a boil. Reduce heat and simmer until syrupy. Serve at room temperature.
- Refrigerate unused marinade up to 1 week. Refrigerate sauce indefinitely.

Uses: On 2 to 3 pounds of chicken (in pieces or skewered), or seafood. Marinate 2 hours.

At Chan Dara Restaurant in Los Angeles, "barbecued chicken" means poultry that's bathed in a curry-spiced, coconut milk marinade before grilling. Owner Ken Kittivech serves it with the traditional Thai accompaniments: green papaya salad, sticky rice and a sweet, hot dip loaded with garlic.

MONGOLIAN MARINADE

David SooHoo is the chef at Chinois East-West, one of Sacramento's hot fusion-style restaurants; his wife, Elaine Corn, writes books aimed at beginner cooks. At home, their cooking styles often intertwine. This family favorite not only contains the Asian flavors they love, but it has another bonus Elaine especially appreciates when she's racing to meet a deadline: It takes less than 5 minutes to make. They use it for lamb chops, the Mongolian meat of choice. We think it dresses up whatever kind of meat we have on hand.

Makes 2 cups

1 cup hoisin sauce
1/2 cup vinegar (rice wine or distilled)
1/2 cup honey
1 tablespoon minced fresh garlic
1 teaspoon sesame oil
1 teaspoon red pepper flakes
1/2 teaspoon ground white pepper

- In a plastic container, combine ingredients.
- Refrigerate unused marinade up to several weeks.

Uses: As a marinade for lamb, beef, pork or chicken. Marinate meat in refrigerator at least 4 hours.

And an order of lightbulbs on the side: Wrestling fans may remember Abdullah the Butcher, the 395-pound "bad man from the Sudan" who ate lightbulbs and raw meat to scare opponents. He's found a related job: running Abdullah the Butcher's House of Ribs and Chinese Food in Atlanta.

Ah Tong's Special Sauce

Makes about 3/4 cup

6 tablespoons Chinese (or Southeast Asian) bean
   paste, mashed, or bean sauce
3 cloves garlic, minced
3 tablespoons soy sauce
1 tablespoon honey
1 tablespoon rice or cider vinegar
3/4 teaspoon red pepper flakes

- In a plastic or glass bowl large enough to hold
  meat, combine ingredients.

Uses: On chicken, duck or any pork.

Asian Barbecued Ribs

- Marinate slab of pork ribs (about 3 pounds) for
  1/2 to 1 hour. Reserve marinade.
- Grill meat over medium coals until done.
- Meanwhile, pour reserved marinade into a small
  saucepan with about 1/2 cup water or stock. Bring
  to a boil. Reduce heat to medium-low, and simmer
  until reduced to desired consistency. Serve on the
  side as a dipping sauce for ribs.

Olivia Wu, a food writer for the *Chicago Sun Times*, is originally from China but spent much of her childhood in Thailand. She was fascinated by her family's cook there, Ah Tong. "She had gold teeth in front, wore a long braid and spoke in argumentative, finger-pointy Cantonese," Olivia remembers. "Her family owned a barbecue stall in Bangkok that was known for its duck. They'd sew this marinade into the cavity of the duck, then hang it vertically to roast. When the duck was served, the marinade was poured out and used for dipping."

Olivia adapted Ah Tong's sauce for outdoor barbecuing. The secret ingredient is Chinese bean paste. "It's all the better," she says, "if the beans are mashed by hand just before combining the ingredients."

Korean Sesame Marinade

Barbecue is big on the Pacific Rim, even if they don't often call it that. Growing up in Hawaii, Eddie Kaai was able to pick and choose from a dozen grilled cuisines. Like many other Hawaiians, he particularly liked the soy-sesame flavors of Korean barbecue. After a long career in restaurants in Honolulu and San Francisco, Eddie moved to Atlanta, where he often serves skewered beef marinated Korean-style.

Makes about 2 1/2 cups

1 1/2 cups soy sauce
5 to 6 cloves garlic, finely minced
3 tablespoons green onion, thinly sliced
1/4 cup packed brown sugar
2 tablespoons sesame oil
2 tablespoons roasted sesame seeds
1 tablespoon maple syrup
1 tablespoon sugar
2 teaspoons grated fresh ginger
1/2 teaspoon cracked black pepper

- In a large bowl, combine ingredients.
- Marinade will keep several weeks in refrigerator (indefinitely if you omit green onion).

Uses: As a marinade and baste for barbecued beef and shrimp. Marinate thinly sliced sirloin roast overnight in refrigerator, thread meat on skewers, and grill.

Den-Chan's Yakitori Sauce

Makes about 1 1/2 cups

1 cup soy sauce (low-sodium sauce may be used)
1 cup mirin (cooking sake or sweet sake)
1/2 cup sake
1 tablespoon minced fresh ginger
1 clove garlic, minced
Optional flavorings: honey, crushed pineapple or
  puréed mango to taste

- In a small saucepan, combine ingredients, and simmer over low heat for 30 to 45 minutes, until slightly syrupy.
- Refrigerate unused sauce up to several weeks.

Uses: Skewer strips or chunks of meat, chicken, seafood or vegetables on bamboo skewers that have been soaked in water for at least 30 minutes. Cook on a hot grill. Dip in yakitori sauce as soon as they are done. If the sauce is too thin to stick to the kebab, grill a few seconds longer, and dip again.

Dennis Lange was an American teacher in Japan when he first tasted yakitori. "I was just walking down the street around quittin' time, and the smell of barbecue permeated everywhere," he says. It was love at first whiff.

In yakitori, a Japanese version of barbecue, chefs grill kebabs of chicken, mushrooms, liver, even buffalo, and dip them in a sauce made from soy and sake. Unlike teriyaki, another Japanese grilling sauce, it contains no vinegar.

Dennis traded in his schoolbooks for an apron and apprenticed at a yakitori restaurant on the southern island of Kyushu. Today he's chef and part-owner of Yakitori Den-Chan (loose translation: Little Dennis) in Atlanta, a traditional yakitori restaurant with a long grill surrounded by a bar so patrons can watch him work. For his sauce, he imports soy sauce from Kyushu. But he says an amateur can make fine yakitori sauce with soy bought in the States.

DIFFERENT TREATS FOR DIFFERENT MEATS

We get a little tired of the endless debate over which meat makes the best barbecue. You know the feud: A Texan proclaims beef brisket the One True 'Cue, then a Georgian jumps up to praise pork and damn beef as so much barbecued wallet, then the Texan calls pig meat greasy and the Georgian calls the Texan greasy, and pretty soon they're barking up each other's family tree.

Enough already. You'd think pigs and cows were the only critters worth cooking. Truth is, there's a whole world of barbecue out there that doesn't go oink or moo.

Different meats often need different sauces. What works for ribs doesn't usually work for fish or oysters or mutton or poultry. A strong meat like goat needs a strong sauce. A delicate flower like salmon could use the caress of oil. Even chicken, America's favorite backyard bird, could profit from something other than the run-of-the-mill tomato-based sauce millions of us unthinkingly brush on every summer. "I don't think tomatoes belong on some of those other meats," says Charlie Knote, author of *Barbecuing and Sausage-Making Secrets.* "There are other sauces that work better."

May we suggest a few?

Paul Newman's Swordfish Marinade

In *Mr. and Mrs. Bridge,* Paul Newman portrayed a prosperous suburban lawyer who is so stiff-collared he can't even loosen up around a barbecue grill. When he tries to play cookout chef, his maid hurries over and warns, "Mr. Bridge, you're aggravating that chicken!"

The real Paul Newman, we're assured, is more comfortable around a grill. At Newman's Own — the for-charity company that makes the salsa, popcorn and, soon, barbecue sauces that bear his name — they say that the actor does terrific backyard burgers and fish. (Just looking at him, we figured he didn't scarf a lot of pigsicles.) This fish marinade, from Cynthia Mitchell of Dunn Loring, Va., won a Newman's Own recipe contest. The judge and jury was none other than Cool Hand Luke himself — or should that be Hot Grill Luke?

Makes about 1 3/4 cups

1 8-ounce bottle ranch dressing (Newman's Own, perhaps?)
1/4 cup dry white wine
2 tablespoons lemon juice
2 tablespoons lime juice
1 tablespoon chopped fresh rosemary
1 tablespoon chopped fresh dill
1 tablespoon minced capers

- In a plastic container, combine ingredients.
- Refrigerate unused marinade up to 2 weeks.

Uses: As a marinade and baste for grilled fish and chicken. Marinate swordfish or other fish steaks 1 hour, turning occasionally. Brush steaks once midway through grilling.

Hogs and hoop skirts: The most famous barbecue scene in the movies (or books, for that matter)? That's easy. In the opening scenes of Gone With the Wind, Scarlett meets Rhett while scores of pigs meet their maker over the coals at Twelve Oaks.

Danny's Baldheaded Seafood Sauce

Makes about 1 2/3 cups

1/2 cup soy sauce
1/3 cup honey or corn syrup
1/3 cup water
1/4 cup packed brown sugar
1/4 cup pineapple juice
Juice of 1 lemon
1/2 teaspoon powdered ginger
1/2 teaspoon garlic powder
1/2 teaspoon ground black pepper
1/2 teaspoon ground red pepper

- In a plastic container, combine ingredients.
- Refrigerate unused marinade up to several weeks.

Uses: As a marinade for seafood, chicken and steak.
Danny marinates shrimp, grouper or scallops for 1
1/2 to 2 hours in refrigerator.

Let's address the obvious question first: No, Danny's sauce will not make your hair fall out. While Danny Guthrie once had a blond ponytail, his saucemaking hobby had nothing to do with the fact that his head now resembles a hard-boiled egg. "My sauce has a kick, but not that much of a kick," he says.

Danny runs an optical lab in Tallahassee, Fla., and sells bottled sauce on the side. His secret ingredient is obviously a sense of humor. The label shows flames rising from his sunburned head, over the slogan: "Smooth taste that shines above the rest."

"I figured people wouldn't tease me if I teased myself first," he says.

They eat a lot of seafood in the Panhandle, so Danny gave us his recipe for a tropical marinade.

Turner Ranch Bison Marinade and Sauce

It wasn't enough for Ted Turner to change the way the world gets its news; he wanted to change the way it eats. Even before he started Cable News Network, the media mogul was breeding bison on his Florida ranch. Now he's owner of America's largest bison herd, most of which roam the plains of his ranch near Bozeman, Mont. The Flying D, he calls the spread. (He once threatened to rename it "Buffalot," after King Arthur's realm.)

Ted's Guinevere, Jane Fonda, says she likes bison meat because it's leaner than beef. The king puts it more bluntly: "You never see a buffalo with fat hanging off its butt like a cow."

Ted and Jane are so fashionably trim, we wondered . . . do they really eat this stuff? Absolutely, says Karen Averitt, their cook at the Flying D. "I never run out to the store for beef or chicken. We eat lots of bison. We'll dig a pit and smoke it Hawaiian style." She's made this dish several times for her famous employers and their guests.

Makes about 3/4 cup

4 cloves garlic, minced
2 shallots, minced
1/2 cup olive oil
1 tablespoon Dijon mustard
1 tablespoon cracked black pepper
1 tablespoon fresh thyme leaves
1/4 cup fresh rosemary

• In a blender, combine ingredients.

Uses: Pour marinade over a tenderloin of bison or beef (or other roast) and marinate for 2 hours to 2 days. Remove meat, reserving marinade. Grill meat over hot coals, searing to seal in moisture.

Serve with Bison Table Sauce: In a small saucepan, combine reserved marinade, 1/2 cup dry sherry, 1/4 cup bison or beef stock, 1/4 cup sun-dried tomato paste (or regular tomato paste) and 2 tablespoons capers. Bring to a boil. Reduce heat to medium, and simmer until sauce is reduced to desired consistency. Refrigerate unused marinade up to 2 weeks. Refrigerate sauce up to several days, or freeze.

For a list of bison suppliers, call the National Bison Association at 303-292-2833. If you don't want to go to the trouble of tracking bison, here's a little secret: Karen's recipe works well on barbecued beef. Don't tell Ted.

FOR-THE-BIRDS PORT-CITRUS GLAZE

Makes about 2 1/2 cups

1/2 cup (1 stick) unsalted butter
1 cup packed brown sugar
1/2 cup orange juice
1/2 cup port wine
Juice of 1 lemon
Salt and pepper to taste

- In a small saucepan, melt butter. Add remaining ingredients. Cook until brown sugar is dissolved.
- Refrigerate unused glaze up to 2 weeks.

Uses: As a glaze for quail, Cornish hen, pheasant, turkey, chicken or other game birds.

To grill and glaze quail: Using kitchen shears, split quail along backbone; flatten the birds by applying pressure on the breast with the palm of your hand. Baste with sauce, and grill over low heat (to keep the sugary glaze from burning), turning and basting every 10 to 15 minutes. Cooking time will vary greatly depending on intensity of heat; it could take longer than an hour.

To broil: Place backside up in broiler pan with no rack. Broil about 5 minutes, 4 to 5 inches from heat. Turn breast side up, and broil another 5 to 10 minutes, or until juices run clear when fork is inserted into meatiest part of breast.

Jane Long runs the Easy Way Out, an Atlanta catering company and gourmet take-out which features many specialties of her native Savannah. A backyard cookout at one of her events would likely include oysters roasted over coals, as well as grilled quail — dressed up for company in an irresistible caramelized, port-infused glaze. "It's wonderful served for brunch with cheese grits and broiled tomatoes," Jane says. "Or you could serve it with wild rice for a fancy dinner party."

KENTUCKY BLACK DIP

Black isn't the first color that comes to mind when you think about barbecue sauce. Motor oil and printer's ink, yes. But barbecue sauce? That's supposed to be some succulent shade of red. "We hear it all the time," says Ken Bosley, proprietor of the Moonlite BBQ Drive-in in Owensboro, Ky. "People see our black dip and say, 'This isn't barbecue sauce.' But they usually like it once they try it."

Owensboro, on the Ohio River in western Kentucky, is the undisputed mutton barbecue capital of the world. You could almost say it's a religion. The tradition started last century when Catholic churches raised money by digging pits, killing sheep and smoking 'em for the Lord. The traditional sheep dip (sorry) served by the Moonlite and other barbecue places around Owensboro goes something like this.

Makes 6 1/2 cups

6 cups water
2/3 cup Worcestershire sauce
2/3 cup distilled vinegar
1 tablespoon lemon juice
1 tablespoon ground black pepper
1/2 tablespoon salt
2 teaspoons packed brown sugar
1/8 teaspoon allspice
1/8 teaspoon garlic powder
1/8 teaspoon onion salt
1/8 teaspoon MSG (optional)

- In a large saucepan, combine ingredients. Bring to a boil. Reduce heat to low, and simmer for 15 minutes.
- Store unused dip indefinitely in a cool, dark place.

Uses: As a mop and dip for mutton. For information on ordering Moonlite dip, see final chapter.

❧

Cueshine: Folklore holds that Kentuckians spike their black dip with white lightning. "Nah," says Ken Bosley of the Moonlite. "We've got moonshine, but we try to save that for the VIPs."

❧

Big Bob Gibson's Alabama White Sauce

Makes about 2 1/4 cups

1 cup mayonnaise
1 cup cider vinegar
1 tablespoon lemon juice
1 1/2 tablespoons cracked black pepper
1/2 teaspoon salt
1/4 teaspoon ground red pepper

- In a plastic container, combine ingredients.
- Refrigerate unused sauce up to several months.

Uses: As a marinade, finishing and dipping sauce for chicken or fish.

This is some funny-looking barbecue sauce. A creamy off-white, with dark speckles, it looks like Miracle Whip caught the measles. But plenty of people in northern Alabama swear by it, and we began to see why when we tried it on barbecued chicken. It tastes like extra-peppery ranch dressing.

No one's quite sure how Big Bob Gibson came to create a mayonnaise-based sauce back in the 1920s. Gibson's five children all went into the barbecue business and spread daddy's dip throughout the Tennessee River Valley. Now you can find it in grocery stores or buy it from the flagship restaurant in Decatur (see final chapter for more information). "Kids put it on bread, potato chips, their fingers," says manager Don McLemore, one of Big Bob's grandsons. We'll stick to the chicken.

CALIFORNIA BARBECUED OYSTERS

A couple of tourists from Georgia were driving along the Pacific Coast Highway north of San Francisco when a hand-painted sign forced their car to the side of the road. "Bar-B-Q Oysters," it blared. Even though they had just eaten lunch, Jim and his wife, Pam, couldn't help it; they had to stop and sample. It was worth the discomfort.

You can find barbecued oysters all along the northern California coast. They're actually grilled, not barbecued. The name refers to the barbecue sauce they simmer in on the half-shell. "Each shell is like a little kettle," explained Joshua Wagle, the grill man at Tony's Seafood, beside Tomales Bay in Marshall, Calif. "It's nothing like the barbecue I had back home in Kansas." No, Joshua, you can't watch them hose down fresh oysters in Kansas. Here's our version of this dish, which uses barbecue sauce, then a garlic-wine sauce.

Makes enough for about 3 dozen oysters

BARBECUE SAUCE

3/4 cup ketchup
1 tablespoon Worcestershire sauce
Juice of 1 lemon
1 teaspoon Dijon mustard
Few dashes hot pepper sauce

GARLIC-WINE SAUCE

4 tablespoons (1/2 stick) butter
1 tablespoon minced garlic
1/4 cup white wine

- In a small bowl, combine barbecue sauce ingredients, and set aside.
- In a small saucepan, combine butter and garlic, and heat until butter melts. Stir in wine.
- Place about 1 teaspoon of barbecue sauce on each oyster, and set them on a hot grill. When the sauce bubbles and oysters begin to curl, add about 1 teaspoon of garlic-wine sauce to each.
- Remove from heat and eat immediately.

DALE'S NEW ORLEANS BARBECUED SHRIMP

Makes 4 servings

2 sticks butter
1 12-ounce can beer
1/4 cup Worcestershire sauce
8 to 10 cloves garlic, mashed
1 tablespoon coarsely ground black pepper
1/2 teaspoon salt (optional)
1/2 teaspoon ground red pepper
About 10 shots Tabasco sauce
1 teaspoon liquid hickory smoke, or to taste
2 pounds large shrimp, heads on

- Preheat oven to 350 degrees. In a large cast-iron skillet or baking pan, melt butter.
- Remove from oven, and add beer, Worcestershire sauce, garlic, peppers, salt, Tabasco and liquid hickory smoke.
- Add shrimp, and cook in oven, uncovered, for about 10 to 20 minutes, stirring occasionally, until shrimp are pink and slightly pulling away from their shells. Do not overcook.
- Have guests peel their own shrimp, and serve plenty of crusty French or Italian bread for sopping.

New Orleans is famous for many great dishes, but barbecue isn't one of them — at least not the kind that involves pig or cow. What you find on menus all over town, though, is some version of barbecued shrimp: large, head-on shrimp baked (yes — in an oven, not on a grill) in a buttery sauce loaded with garlic and spices. The idea originated in the 1950s at Pascal's Manale restaurant, where it remains the house specialty. "The shrimp gives it a color that looks like barbecue sauce, but it doesn't taste like barbecue sauce," says chef Mark Defelice, grandson of the dish's creator, Pascal Radosta.

OK, so it ain't barbecue. But it makes a great sauce and a great party centerpiece. As with any sauce, every cook has a favorite recipe. Ours comes from Dale Curry, who has tried most of them as food editor of the *Times-Picayune* in New Orleans. The key ingredient? "Shrimp heads," she says. "The fat from the heads cooks into the sauce."

TROPICAL BARBECUE SAUCE FOR SHRIMP

Frankly, we can think of a lot of things this would be good with, but its fruity, fiery, tropical flavors lend themselves particularly well to shrimp. No wonder customers can't get enough of it at New York's popular Sugar Reef Caribbean restaurant where it was created. (Actually, this is a somewhat milder version of the one that appears in Devra Dedeaux's *The Sugar Reef Cookbook* — and we don't consider ourselves wimps when it comes to spices.)

Makes about 1 quart

1/4 cup vegetable oil
1/4 cup packed brown sugar
1 medium white onion, chopped
1 medium red onion, chopped
3 cloves garlic, minced
1 large orange, peeled, seeded and chopped
1 29-ounce can tomato sauce
1 5-ounce bottle Pickapeppa sauce
Juice of 2 lemons
2 tablespoons ground cumin
1 tablespoon coarsely ground black pepper
1 tablespoon ground white pepper
1/4 teaspoon ground red pepper
Marinade reserved from shrimp (optional; recipe to follow)
Tabasco sauce to taste (optional)

- In a large saucepan, heat oil over medium heat. Add brown sugar, and stir constantly until sugar melts and begins to caramelize.
- Add onions and garlic, and sauté 1 minute. Add orange, and let mixture simmer for 10 minutes over medium-low heat.
- Add tomato sauce, Pickapeppa sauce and lemon juice. Continue to cook over medium-low heat until sauce begins to thicken.
- Add cumin and peppers, and simmer 5 to 10 minutes longer.
- Sauce may be made up to several weeks ahead at this point, covered and refrigerated.

- Before using, add marinade reserved from shrimp and hot sauce, if desired. Cook long enough to heat through.

TROPICAL MARINADE

Makes about 1 1/4 cups

4 cloves garlic, minced
2 green onions, finely chopped
Juice of 4 oranges
1/4 cup Worcestershire sauce

- In a large plastic or glass bowl, combine ingredients.

Uses: Cubed pork or chicken would work well in both the sauce and marinade, but shrimp is its true match.

TROPICAL SHRIMP

- In a large container, combine marinade and 3 pounds large, peeled and deveined shrimp. Cover, and refrigerate at least 1 hour.
- Place shrimp on skewers, alternating with chunks of onion, green pepper and peeled orange.
- Grill over hot coals for about 5 minutes per side, liberally basting with the barbecue sauce.
- Serve with extra sauce on the side.

We're No. 1! Which state is most barbecue-crazy? Judging by the number of barbecue sauces produced, it'd have to be North Carolina. Its agriculture department promotes 51 locally made sauces; a similar program in Texas promotes 28.

Lemonade Chicken Baste

Some of the best chicken marinates are the simplest. In Maine, for instance, they coat chicken in a mixture that's 3 parts cider vinegar, 2 parts water and 1 part vegetable oil (with salt and pepper to taste) — a marinade that seems as natural to us as a white church steeple against a blue New England sky. This baste, from the National Broiler Council, is a little more involved but similar in its straightforwardness. It's all about lemons . . .

Makes about 3 3/4 cups

1 12-ounce can frozen lemonade concentrate
1 cup ketchup
1/2 cup cider vinegar
1/4 cup vegetable oil
1/4 cup soy sauce
2 tablespoons packed brown sugar
2 tablespoons Worcestershire sauce
1 tablespoon yellow mustard
1 teaspoon garlic powder
1 teaspoon celery salt
1/2 teaspoon salt

- In a medium saucepan, combine ingredients. Bring to a boil. Remove from heat.
- Refrigerate unused sauce up to 2 weeks.

Uses: As a finishing and table sauce for chicken — though it would also pair well with pork, shrimp or other seafood. Baste chicken, and serve leftover sauce (reheated to kill bacteria) on the side.

North-to-Alaska Salmon Brine and Rub

Brine

Makes about 4 1/2 cups

2 cups soy sauce
1 cup dry white wine
1 cup water
1/3 cup packed brown sugar
1/4 cup non-iodized salt
1/2 teaspoon onion powder
1/2 teaspoon garlic powder
1/2 teaspoon ground black pepper
1/2 teaspoon Tabasco sauce

• In a plastic container, combine ingredients.

Dry Rub

Makes about 2 cups

1 cup packed brown sugar
1 cup non-iodized salt
3/4 teaspoon garlic powder
1/2 teaspoon onion powder
1/2 teaspoon ground white pepper

• In a bowl, combine ingredients.

Uses: On salmon and other fish. Marinate up to 8 hours, refrigerated. Or roll fish in rub and refrigerate 4 hours. Rinse and pat dry before grilling or smoking. Don't use marinade and rub.

Orris and Ruby Presley lived in Alaska for 17 years before retiring to his old homeplace near Eatonton, Ga. They see a lot of deer and possums in the Georgia woods; they saw a lot of caribou and grizzlies in the Alaska wilds. Orris, an avid outdoorsman, soon got bored and was itching to go back.

So every year the Presleys drive 5,002 miles to visit their children in Alaska and indulge their passion for wilderness. The long summer daylight affords Orris more time to fish for salmon, which he cleans and ships frozen back to Georgia. By the time they return in the fall, as much as 250 pounds of Alaska salmon is waiting for them. They like to brine it or give it a dry rub, then cure it for 8 hours in their electric smoker. We tasted the end result, and let's just say a river runs through it.

George 'n' Ginger Venison Marinade

When we spoke to Thomas Henry Nickerson, an Atlanta attorney and hunter, he had just taken a call from a sportswriter who wanted his recipe for jellied moose lips. We suspect Thomas Henry was serving us baloney. But who knows? The man has a million stories — and recipes. "Bushels full of them," he says. "I'm getting ready to eat corned bear on rye right now." We'll settle for this spirited marinade, which Thomas Henry uses on the venison he hauls out of the Georgia woods.

Makes about 2 cups

3/4 cup raspberry ginger ale
1/2 cup George Dickel sour mash whiskey
1/2 cup lemon juice
1/4 cup soy sauce
2 cloves garlic, crushed
2 tablespoons sugar
1 teaspoon salt
1 teaspoon ground black pepper

- In a plastic container, combine ingredients.
- Refrigerate unused marinade up to several weeks.

Uses: As marinade for venison or other large game. Also works great for beef cuts that could stand a little tenderizing, such as flank steak. Marinate at least 6 hours or overnight.

Northwestern Low-Acid Marinade and Mop

Makes about 1 1/2 cups

1/2 cup bourbon or sherry
1/4 cup soy sauce
1/4 cup vegetable oil
1/4 cup peanut oil
3 tablespoons sesame oil
2 teaspoons Worcestershire sauce
2 teaspoons garlic powder
Ground black pepper to taste

- In a small saucepan, combine ingredients over low heat, and simmer 15 minutes.
- Store unused marinade indefinitely in a cool, dark place.

Uses: As a marinade and baste on beef and poultry. The Beavers love to hunt and also use it on fish and game.

Other meats we passed up: In the cult classic Night of the Living Dead, zombies gnaw on freshly barbecued human. Like many Texans, they don't mess with sauce.

Almost every barbecue sauce contains either tomatoes or vinegar. That's bad news if your stomach won't let you do acid. Here's a low-acid alternative from a Northwestern cook-off team with a very odd name.

The Beaver Castors of Bellevue, Wash., took their name from a scent gland in beavers that produces a strong, oily substance used in some perfumes. Relax, there's none of it in this recipe. They don't even put it on beaver meat, as far as we know.

The Beavers do know their barbecue. They won the award for best sauce at the 1993 Jack Daniel's contest. Chief cook Jim Erickson, a tool salesman, came up with this concoction. It doesn't taste great by itself, but it does wonders when it gets to know a piece of meat.

Barney McBee's Texas Goat Sauce

It's a question that has bedeviled epicures for years: what to serve with smoked goat? If anyone has the answer it's the people of Brady, Texas, a town that prides itself on being the geographic heart of the Lone Star State — as well as the heart of its goat-raising region.

For over 20 years this small town has staged the World Championship Barbeque Goat Cook-off. It isn't just a novelty; a lot of people in southern Texas and Mexico eat cabrito, as they call barbecued goat. "It's a little coarser and gamier than beef, but it's sure better than mutton," says Kathy Roddie Johnson, who helps run the contest for the chamber of commerce.

One of the masters of barbecued goat was Barney McBee, a two-time champion who ran a cafe in nearby Comanche. Barney died a few years ago but was good enough to bequeath his neighbors the recipe for his secret goat sauce, which originated half a century ago with his mother-in-law, Claudia Ake. Now that's a family that knows the meaning of citizenship.

Makes about 7 cups

1/2 cup vegetable oil
2 onions, chopped
1 clove garlic, mashed
1 32-ounce bottle ketchup
3 tablespoons yellow mustard
2 cups black coffee
1 cup distilled vinegar
1 lemon, cut in half
6 tablespoons chili powder
3 good taps Worcestershire sauce
Salt and pepper to taste

- In a large saucepan, heat oil over medium-low heat. Add onions and garlic, and sauté until tender but not brown.
- In a large bowl, whisk together ketchup and mustard, and add to saucepan, along with remaining ingredients.
- Simmer over low heat for 1 hour.
- Refrigerate unused sauce up to several weeks.

Uses: While it's meant for goat, this sauce has an earthy flavor (probably from the coffee) that goes nicely with beef or mutton.

WHERE'S-THE-BEEF TOFU MARINADE

Makes about 1 cup

1/2 cup Major Grey's mango chutney
2 tablespoons sun-dried tomato paste concentrate
1/3 cup lemon juice
1/3 cup olive oil
2 jalapeño peppers, seeded and minced
3 garlic cloves, minced
Cracked black pepper to taste

- In a blender or food processor fitted with steel blade, combine chutney, tomato paste and lemon juice, and purée.
- With motor running, drizzle in oil a little at a time. Mix in jalapeño, and garlic. Season with pepper.
- Refrigerate unused marinade up to 2 weeks.

Uses: As a marinade for grilled tofu. We cheated and used it on chicken, and suspect it'd be great on fish and even meat. (If you're grilling tofu, make sure it's well-drained and the grill top is well oiled. Tofu is delicate and can fall apart if you're not careful.)

Yeah, we know: This is supposed to be a chapter about different meats. So we fibbed this once. We'd be the first to agree that everything tastes better on a grill, and something as bland as tofu needs all the help it can get. So for our herbivore friends, we offer this vibrant marinade — inspired by Jim Tarantino's *Marinades* — that makes even tofu enticing. Tofu also pairs well with soy-heavy sauces in this book, such as Secret Asian Sauce on page 95 and Korean Sesame Marinade on 108.

Who says barbecue is just for carnivores?

DRY RUBS

*G*rowing up in the Southeast, we never heard much about rubs. We were taught that you put sauce on barbecue — and maybe a little coleslaw — but nothing else. Rubs? Why would anyone in their right mind put Vick's Vapo-Rub on a piece of meat that wasn't attached to their body?

Then, as an Ole Miss coed, Susan made the pilgrimage to Charlie Vergos' Rendezvous in Memphis, where they serve fall-off-the-bone unsauced dry ribs. And then Jim started noticing how the best cook-off teams all seem to use rubs in addition to sauce, lovingly patting their pork like mamas powdering a baby's behind. We were converted.

Dry rubs are those magical mixtures of spice and seasoning that seal in moisture and caramelize into a crusty bark with a bite. Barbecue masters have always prepped with the most rudimentary rub, salt and pepper. Now it's common to see mixtures with more than 10 ingredients.

Nowhere are rubs used more widely than Texas. Texans have been known to get defensive in their dealings with the sauce-centric world outside the Republic. "Ask a Texan for sauce," says Dallas barbecue cook Obie Obermark, "and you've just told him his meat was dry."

We'd think twice about telling any Texan that. But with rubs, the subject rarely comes up.

RON'S REAL GOOD RUB

Jim first saw him bent over a cooker in a parking lot near the Dallas-Fort Worth airport. He looked like a Texas barbecue man ought to look — big and beefy, with a black cowboy hat, thick sagebrush on his upper lip and a belt buckle large enough to carve a steak on. He reached into the smoker and pulled out a hunk of something swaddled in scorched foil. "Here," he said, "I'll bet you never had brisket like this in Georgia." Jim hadn't.

Ron Robason heads the International Barbecue Cookers Association, a fancy name for the organization that sponsors most of the cook-offs in north Texas. Like most of its 350 members, he believes the ultimate barbecue is a beef brisket patted down with dry rub and smoked over indirect heat for seven hours. It was a tender, moist revelation to a Georgian accustomed to the dried-out carcass that passes for beef barbecue in pig country.

Ron wants to spread the word about Texas barbecue. His rub should help. If it seems salty at first, don't worry; all that smoke and dripping absolutely transform it.

Makes 1 cup

1/4 cup salt
2 tablespoons paprika
2 tablespoons MSG (optional)
4 teaspoons ground black pepper
4 teaspoons ground red pepper
4 teaspoons chili powder
4 teaspoons granulated garlic
4 teaspoons lemon pepper
4 teaspoons ground coriander

- Combine ingredients in small container. Store in a cool, dry place (as with all rubs unless otherwise noted).

Uses: On cow, of course. Ron pats the rub onto meat 30 minutes before cooking. Apply again midway through smoking. He also puts it on chicken and pork ribs, glazing with honey a few minutes before taking them off the grill.

A note about MSG: Many rub recipes use the flavor enhancer monosodium glutamate. Some people are sensitive to MSG and blame it for nausea and dizziness — the so-called "Chinese food syndrome." If MSG rubs you the wrong way, eliminate it. Or you can reduce the amount.

Scott's South-Meets-South-of-France Rub

Makes about 7 tablespoons

2 tablespoons packed light brown sugar
1 tablespoon sea salt
1 1/2 teaspoons crushed dried rosemary
1 teaspoon cracked black pepper
1 teaspoon dried thyme, crushed (Scott uses Spice
   Island)
3/4 teaspoon ground cumin
1/2 teaspoon ground oregano
1/2 teaspoon ground cardamom
1/4 teaspoon ground coriander
1/4 teaspoon ground cinnamon
1/4 teaspoon powdered ginger
1/4 teaspoon sweet Hungarian paprika
1 small bay leaf, finely crumbled
4 cloves garlic, minced to a paste

• Combine ingredients. Refrigerate unused rub up
  to several weeks.

Uses: Rub on leg of lamb before grilling, smoking or
roasting. Also good with chicken, beef and pork.

Scott Peacock never misses an opportunity to promote Southern cooking. His interpretations of classic Southern fare have made the Horseradish Grill one of Atlanta's most popular restaurants. Along with his mentor, Southern cooking authority Edna Lewis, he co-founded the Society for the Revival and Preservation of Southern Food. The roots of this particular rub, however, are not in Southern history but in the Alabama-born chef's pantry.

"I was experimenting with smoked lamb and just started pulling things out and mixing them together. I think subconsciously I got the idea from the spice mixture [French cooking teacher] Madeleine Kamman made for her duck confit when I was in her class. But really, if you consult the old Southern cookbooks like *The Carolina Housewife*, you'll find those aromatic spices used in many of the dishes."

So, deep down, this rub's got a Southern accent? Sounds like a stretch to us, Scott. We're including it not because of where it came from but because it tastes great.

OL' HAWG'S BREATH

Who would have thought Al Gore had hawg's breath? The vice president, a rib man from way back, has cooked at Memphis in May several times with the Washington Pigskins team. When the government porkers come to the banks of the Mississippi, they join forces with a local team sponsored by Schering-Plough HealthCare Products, Ol' Hawg's Breath. The captain, Lewis Nolan, sent us this sugary rub, which has been spotted — smeared and greasy — on the face of the man who's just a heartbeat away.

Makes about 1 cup

3 tablespoons sugar
3 tablespoons lemon pepper
3 tablespoons paprika
3 tablespoons dry barbecue seasoning
2 tablespoons MSG (optional)
1 teaspoon garlic powder
1 teaspoon ground red pepper
1 teaspoon ground cinnamon
1/2 teaspoon ground nutmeg

Uses: On pork ribs and shoulders.

OBIE'S TEXAS SOL RUB

Makes 1 cup

5 tablespoons paprika
2 1/2 tablespoons salt
2 tablespoons garlic powder
2 tablespoons onion powder
4 teaspoons ground black pepper
4 teaspoons dried parsley
2 teaspoons ground red pepper
2 teaspoons ground cumin
1 teaspoon ground coriander
1 teaspoon dried oregano
1/4 teaspoon powdered jalapeño (widely available in
    Texas and the Southwest; it's also good without it)

Uses: On beef. It works beautifully with the brisket-
smoking recipe in the introductory chapter.

Obie Obermark — Texan, Deadhead, barbecue man — offers this helpful tip for telling when your brisket is done: "If it feels like you're pressing on a good firm beer belly, it's done. If it feels like a blob of jelly, put it back on." If no beer bellies are available (we know, fat chance), substitute a firm buttock — if you dare. Here's a great rub from Obie. Naturally, he douses his brisket with beer.

❧

Das what? In Das Barbecü, a musical staged in New York in 1994, Wagner's "Ring" cycle of operas was recast around feuding Texas families. During the big number, two jilted brides, who were to have been married at a barbecue, get sauce all over their white dresses as they eat away their sorrows.

❧

MIDLAND TOO BRISKET RUB

Like a lot of Texans, Jerry King was a chilihead. But the deeper he got into the chili cook-off circuit, the more he began to see the darker side of that fevered obsession. "It was too political," he says. "Those people would kill their mother to win a championship."

Jerry, a trucking supervisor in Odessa, soon switched allegiance to barbecue, where the people generally conducted themselves according to the pit man's credo: low and slow, avoid flare-ups. Team Midland Too, Jerry's cooking crew, created this somewhat sweet rub. It's one of the few we've seen with dry mustard.

Makes 1 1/3 cups

4 tablespoons sugar
3 tablespoons onion powder
3 tablespoons salt
2 tablespoons dry mustard
2 tablespoons paprika
2 tablespoons ground black pepper
2 tablespoons granulated garlic
2 tablespoons MSG (optional)
1 tablespoon onion salt
1 teaspoon ground cumin
1 teaspoon celery salt

Uses: On beef. Rub on brisket 30 minutes to an hour before cooking. Spritz brisket with apple juice every hour during 5- to 7-hour smoking time. During the last hour of cooking, wrap in foil to collect juices, which make an excellent natural sauce.

❧

Czexans: Many people in central Texas are of Czech descent. The link is so strong that when a living history museum opened in the Czech town of Roznov, they dug Eastern Europe's first authentic Texas barbecue pit.

❧

RICK'S OKLAHOMA-CHICAGO-MEXICO RUB

Makes 2 2/3 cups

2/3 cup paprika
1/3 cup kosher salt
1/3 cup sugar
1/3 cup packed brown sugar
1/3 cup ground New Mexican chili powder
1/3 cup ground cumin
1/3 cup ground black pepper

Uses: On meats, game, poultry, fish or vegetables. Particularly good on swordfish, tuna and portabello mushrooms.

Give us a break: The McRib sandwich wasn't the only stab McDonald's made at barbecue. The chain introduced a hamburger slathered in barbecue sauce at its Chicago franchises in 1991. The name? McJordan, after you-know-who.

When you think of Chicago barbecue, you usually think of all those rib shacks that keep the Southside in a pleasant haze. But there are other things smoking on the shores of Lake Michigan. Some of the most creative barbecue comes from Rick Bayless of Topolobampo and the Frontera Grill, a chef and cookbook author who's best known as an authority on Mexican cuisine. This particular recipe has its roots a little farther north. Rick comes from Oklahoma, where his parents run a barbecue joint and people would just as soon use a rub as a sauce. Rick's version, which first appeared in *Food Arts* magazine, has lots of chili powder.

Zup's Porchetta Rub

This pork rub comes from Jim Zupancich, co-owner of Zup's Food Market in the northern Minnesota town of Ely. Founded in 1916, Zup's has been selling its popular porchetta roasts, already seasoned and salted, for many years. The rub has its roots in Italy, where porchetta refers to a whole roasted pig coated in black pepper and fennel seeds. It's often sold as sandwiches in groceries with signs that advertise "Porchetta Oggi" ("Porchetta Today"). The salt rub, by the way, tastes great by itself on beef roasts.

Seasoning Rub

Makes about 1 cup

3 tablespoons fennel seed
2 tablespoons dried celery flakes
2 tablespoons celery seed
2 tablespoons dried parsley
2 tablespoons dried basil
2 tablespoons dried rosemary
2 tablespoons dried oregano

Salt Rub

Makes 6 tablepoons

2 tablespoons non-iodized salt
2 tablespoons onion salt
1 tablespoon ground black pepper
1 tablespoon cracked black pepper

• Combine ingredients for seasoning rub and salt rub separately.

Uses: On pork butt roast, tenderloin or pork chops. Roll meat in the seasonings to coat, then sprinkle salt mixture all over to taste. Roast or grill. Delicious hot or in cold sandwiches.

CHARLIE'S ZAP II RUB

Makes about 6 tablespoons

1 tablespoon sugar
1 tablespoon packed brown sugar
1 1/2 tablespoons salt
1 tablespoon ground sage
1 1/2 teaspoons paprika
1 1/2 teaspoons ground thyme
1 1/2 teaspoons ground oregano
1 1/2 teaspoons garlic powder
1 1/2 teaspoons ground black pepper
1/4 teaspoon MSG (optional)

Uses: On pork. Rub in 1 1/2 tablespoons per pound, letting meat stand for 2 hours at room temperature or 72 hours in refrigerator.

"I'm a great one for rubs," says barbecue master Charlie Knote of Cape Girardeau, Mo. "They solve a lot of problems, and they're easier to work with than sauce." Charlie gives his rubs cute little names like Zip, Zep and Zap (no relation to Zup). He calls this sagey creation Zap II because it has twice as much zap.

Bed of coals: The earliest citation for barbecue in the Oxford English Dictionary comes from 1661. One early meaning was "a rude wooden frame-work, used in America for sleeping on."

Meat junkies: Some competitive cooks have taken to injecting meat with sauce and other liquids. Ron Robason, who runs a Texas cook-off circuit, main-lines his chicken with peppermint schnapps.

CAJUN

Makes about 1/4 cup
1 tablespoon cracked black pepper
1 tablespoon ground white pepper
1 tablespoon salt
2 teaspoons paprika
1 teaspoon granulated garlic
1 teaspoon onion powder
1/2 teaspoon ground red pepper

Uses: On fish, chicken, hamburgers and anything else that could use a little blackening.

INDIAN

Makes about 1/4 cup
1 tablespoon ground cumin
1 tablespoon garam marsala (a spice mixture available at Indian markets)
2 teaspoons ground coriander
1 teaspoon salt
1 teaspoon red pepper flakes
1 teaspoon cracked black pepper

Uses: On chicken, lamb or shrimp.

JAMAICAN

Makes about 1/3 cup
2 tablespoons onion powder
2 teaspoons sugar
2 teaspoons ground thyme

2 teaspoons salt
1 1/2 teaspoons ground red pepper
1 teaspoon coarsely ground black pepper
1 teaspoon allspice
1/4 teaspoon ground cinnamon

Uses: On fish, chicken and vegetables.

MEDITERRANEAN

Makes about 1/3 cup
1 tablespoon fresh or 1 teaspoon dried each: thyme,
   rosemary, sage, marjoram
1 tablespoon minced garlic
1/2 teaspoon kosher salt
1/4 teaspoon cracked black pepper

Uses: On beef. To use on fish, add grated zest of one
lemon. Squeeze lemon juice on fish with rub.

MEXICAN

Makes about 1/3 cup
2 tablespoons chili powder
1 tablespoon salt
2 teaspoons ground red pepper
2 teaspoons ground cumin
1 teaspoon garlic powder
1 teaspoon ground coriander

Uses: On beef, pork or poultry.

That's entertainment: At the Memphis in May cook-off one year, the Pot-Bellied Porkers team tried to impress judges by removing their shirts, painting red lips around their navels and rippling their bellies in time to "The Colonel Bogie March." Said one member, "I don't think that won us any points."

Kreuz Market's We-Don't-Need-No-Stinkin'-Sauce Rub

Man. Meat. Fire. It doesn't get more basic than Kreuz Market, one of the oldest barbecue joints in Texas. Located in Lockhart, near San Antonio, Kreuz (rhymes with bites) is a throwback to the late 1800s when America's first commercial barbecue pits appeared in Central Texas. Every town seemed to have a meat market run by a German or Czech family; they're the ones who figured out that people would buy less-choice cuts of meat as long as they were smoked. Before then, barbecue referred to a social gathering where a pig or some other animal was roasted, not to a slow-smoked meat you could buy at a store or restaurant.

Kreuz has been barbecuing sausage and beef shoulders since the turn of the century. You enter through a long, dark, smoky hallway and half expect to see a caveman basting a side of stegosaurus. At the end of the hall there's a fire right out on the open floor — no pit enclosure at all — and a 35-foot chimney drawing smoke over racks of meat. You belly up to the counter and tell the butcher how many slices or links you want. He whacks some off, weighs it and slaps it on a piece of wax paper. Then you repair to a knife-scarred table where strangers share a communal cleaver attached to a chain. Don't ask for a fork; there aren't any. Unless you want to go hungry, you're soon up to your elbows in grease as you use your fingers, your nose, anything to subdue the meat. But it's so good that you forget about the lack of silverware and finish your feast with a long, satisfied, Neanderthal grunt.

The only condiment Kreuz serves is hot pepper sauce. "I don't have anything against barbecue sauce," says Don Schmidt, one of the brothers who runs the place, "but we don't believe it's necessary. I wouldn't know how to make a barbecue sauce."

What Kreuz uses instead is a rub that's almost prehistoric in its simplicity. Here's the formula:

1 part ground black pepper
1 part salt
Ground red pepper to taste

Not much of a recipe, is it? We're kind of embarrassed looking at it. But you definitely can tell it's there on the beef because of the peppery bark it forms. This rub also captures the essential Texas attitude toward barbecue: Let the meat speak for itself.

HERE'S WHAT YOU CAN DO WITH YOUR SAUCE

Barbecue sauce isn't just for barbecue. None other than Elvis knew this; one of his favorite takeout meals was barbecue pizza, a pie topped with sauce and pulled pork. Here are some other uses for sauce:

Dip. Mix with sour cream, yogurt or whipped cream cheese.

Roasted onions. Core a whole sweet onion and fill the cavity with a little sauce; wrap in foil and bake or grill until soft.

Meatloaf. Substitute for ketchup or tomato sauce.

Overstuffed potato. Top a baked potato with shredded beef or chicken tossed in barbecue sauce; add shredded cheddar cheese and sour cream.

Chili. Add barbecue sauce to cooked ground beef or turkey; season with chili powder and red pepper. Add a can of drained beans if you like.

Tacos. Cook ground beef or turkey in a skillet; add barbecue sauce and heat. Spoon into taco shells; add cheese, lettuce, shredded cheese and sour cream.

Bloody Marys. Season with a splash of a vinegary barbecue sauce.

Red coleslaw. Mix equal parts barbecue sauce (tomato or vinegar-based) and mayonnaise; sweeten to taste with a little sugar. Toss with shredded cabbage.

Chicken wings. Heat and mix together equal parts barbecue sauce and melted butter; season to taste with hot pepper sauce. Grill or broil wings, basting with sauce.

Baked beans. Add sauce to canned beans and heat.

Meatballs. Bring equal parts sauce and beef broth to a boil, add meatballs, cover and reduce heat to a simmer until cooked through, about 10 minutes. Remove meatballs, skim fat and boil sauce until it's reduced by about half. Pour over the meatballs.

BY THE BOTTLE

Saucemakers tend to be sauce collectors, and not just for the taste of it. Half the fun is what's on the bottle, not what's in it.

We've seen raging bulls, charging razorbacks, fire-breathing dragons and whole pens full of pigs playing fiddle and dancing about like they're just so happy to be roasted alive. We've licked lips over sauces that are bone-suckin', rib-ticklin', tongue-tinglin' and one that claims to be incendiary enough to set off an atomic bomb. We've met Bubba, Big Bob, Billy Bones, Billy Blues and a few people we already knew had sauces, like Richard Petty, Waylon Jennings, the late Sammy Davis Jr. and, coming soon, Paul Newman.

And then there was the Georgia sauce that said, "No MSG — but lots of love." Touching.

Consumer Reports magazine counted more than 500 commercially bottled barbecue sauces in 1991. We figure the number has ballooned since then. If you're lucky, you'll find a couple of dozen varieties at your grocery store. If you turn the page, you'll find a lot more available by catalog, mail-order or in specialty food shops.

We tasted more than 150 brands and chose 50 of the best. This assemblage of sauce puzzled the delivery man and amused our friends. Gaping at Jim's bottle-studded kitchen, our colleague Al Clayton shook his head and said, "You have taken this to its logical conclusion."

Not really. There's always another sauce out there.

Annie's. A New England sauce that's sweet enough for pancakes, with molasses, brown rice syrup and (surprise) maple syrup. Foster Hill Road, North Calais, Vt. 05650. 802-456-8866.

Arthur Bryant's. The famous Kansas City smokehouse has one of the oddest sauces in barbecue. Its grainy texture, off-red color and unsweet taste turn some people off. But plenty of others get addicted. Harry Truman loved it, hence their slogan: "The President's Choice." 816-231-1123.

Atlanta Burning. General Sherman would have loved this flamethrower. There are no doubt hotter barbecue sauces, but this habañero scorcher had us retreating to the milk jug. Chili-heads will love it. Redwine Farms, 3781 Happy Valley Circle, Newnan, Ga. 30263. 404-253-8100.

Atomic Bob's. The label says it all: a mushroom cloud climbing above a kettle cooker. There are hotter sauces in the Southwest, but this marriage of tomatoes and habañero peppers has a lingering kick. Radiation perhaps? 1010 S. Farley St., Pampa, Texas 79065. 806-665-7755.

BBQ Sauce from Hell. The habañeros are hot enough, but it's the packaging that caught our eye: a cartoon devil among flames of damnation, topped by a classy wax seal. Southwest Specialty Food, 5805 W. McClellan, No. 3, Glendale, Ariz. 85301. 800-536-3131.

Big Bob Gibson Original White Sauce. Here it is, the weirdest barbecue sauce in the land — that mayonnaise-pepper stuff Alabamians love on chicken. 1715 6th Ave. S.E., Decatur, Ala. 35601. 205-350-6969.

Billy Bones. "It took me 16 years to get this sauce right," says William "Billy Bones" Wall, one of the bona fide showmen of the barbecue circuit. This smoky, peppery tomato sauce was worth the time. 751 Saginaw Road, Sanford, Mich. 48657. 517-687-7880.

Bone Suckin' Sauce. Sometimes you buy a bottle just for the name. How can you resist this one out of Raleigh, N.C.? The sweet, tomato-based contents are pretty good, too. 800-446-0947.

Bourbon Q. You can really taste the whiskey in this thin, brown baste and dip out of Louisville. Jack Daniel's, Maker's Mark and most other Kentucky and Tennessee distilleries also have barbecue sauces. Kentucky Cookout Co., P.O. Box 448, Pewee Valley, Ky. 40056. 502-241-2622.

Brother Juniper's Holy Smoke. Yeah, this dark sauce is smoky, but what hooked us was the spicy pepper mash. 463 Sebastopol Ave., Santa Rosa, Calif. 95401. 707-542-9012.

Bubba Q. Some people think barbecue tastes better when it's cooked by someone named Bubba. In that case, South Carolina is set. They've got a lot of Bubbas; they even have a BubbaFest in the town of Sugar Tit. This supertart vinegar sauce should help 'em keep their twang. Atlantis Coastal Foods, 708 King St., Charleston, S.C. 29403. 800-972-2533.

Corky's. Voted Memphis' best barbecue several times in local polls, this restaurant chain is opening in other Southern cities. Its well-balanced, sweetish tomato sauce makes a nice calling card. 5500 Poplar Ave., Bldg D, Suite 2, Memphis, Tenn. 38119. 800-926-7597.

Country's Back Fire. Part Carolina, part Caribbean, this peppery mustard sauce is actually from Georgia. It's hotter than Georgia asphalt, as they say. Country's Barbecue, 2016 12th Ave., Columbus, Ga. 31901. 706-324-5859.

Crazy Cajun. With ingredients like Tabasco sauce, file and brewed Community coffee, is there any doubt where this spicy topping comes from? How about California? The Cajun moved. P.O. Box 426, Petaluma, Calif. 94953. 707-769-8515.

Crazy Jerry's Swine Wine. Jerry Gualtieri does things backasswards. He comes up with a name and a label, then comes up with a sauce. Swine Wine, a mustardy pork bath that's a tad salty, has one of the best labels we saw: a sun-bathing pig lathering himself with sauce. Quoth the Crazy Man: "It's all about packaging and marketing, son." Available in catalogs; for information, 800 347 2823.

Crazy Jim's. Sauce or relish? Jim Igo's recipe is a regular hamburger helper, with its sweet pickle relish and bacon bits. P.O. Box 321, White Horse Beach, Mass. 02381. 508-224-8400.

Danny's Baldheaded Sauce. The thick, brown sugary sauce is fine, but the label is hilarious. It shows Danny's barren dome bursting into flames. The perfect sauce for men who have nothing. P.O. Box 15702, Tallahassee, Fla. 32317. 904-566-4628.

Dragon's Breath. Is that what you get when you eat mustard sauce? A distinctive Carolina yellow with a dragon grilling a drumstick on the label. Three Dots Co., 1707 N. Chestnut St., Lumberton, N.C. 28358. 800-215-5422. (PIN 3183).

Dreamland. Tangy, with a sinus-clearing kick, the sauce John "Big Daddy" Bishop uses at his Alabama rib shack has an avid nationwide following. 800-752-0544.

El Paso Chile Co.Tequila Sauce. This red stuff has a nice jolt, but we never found the worm in the jar. They also make a beer barbecue sauce. 909 Texas Ave., El Paso, Texas 79901. 800-274-7468.

Fenn's Famous Basting Sauce. Burgundy, spice and everything nice. An unusual taste with hints of apple butter. Fenn Little, a former lawyer, makes the sauce; his wife, artist Ruth Lansdell Barrett, hand-paints the labels. 3177 Roswell Road, Atlanta, Ga. 30305. 800-493-3667.

Gate's. What a bright, sunny traipse to the tomato patch this is. Gate's Barbecue, a Kansas City institution, markets several sauces in grocery stores. We love the beautifully balanced original. 4707 The Paseo, Kansas City, Mo. 64110. 800-662-RIBS (800-662-7427).

Hawaiian Passion. With its profusion of peppers and pineapple, this stuff will give you the tropical tinglies. 800-767-4650.

Johnny Harris. The venerable Savannah restaurant makes a mustard-ketchup sauce with lots of pepper. 2801 Wicklow St., Savannah, Ga. 31404. 912-354-8828.

Lime-Time Grilling Sauce. A postcard from Margaritaville. This lime-cilantro-jalapeño marinade cries out for seafood. Hot Sauce Harry's, 3422 Flair Drive, Dallas, Texas 75229. 214-902-8552.

Maurice's Carolina Gold. Maurice Bessinger's Piggie Park makes the nation's best-known mustard sauce. Maurice also does a tomato sauce but signals what he thinks of tomato-eaters by calling it Yankee Red. P.O. Box 6847, West Columbia, S.C. 29171. 800-628-7423.

McClard's. President Clinton's old hangout. Its thin, sweet, mildly hot sauce has one of the best-known stories in barbecue. Back in the 1920s, it seems, a man skipped out of the McClard family's tourist court without paying his bill. He left a note with a sauce recipe instead — the same recipe they use today. True or not, it's a good story. 103 River Bend Drive, Hot Springs, Ark. 71913. 501-767-4063.

Moonlite Bar-B-Q Dip. The pits of Owensboro, Ky., barbecue 20,000 pounds of mutton a week, half of it at the Moonlite. The drive-in makes more traditional tomato sauces, but this thin, Worcestershire-laced dip is what they use on mutton. 2840 W. Parrish Ave., Owensboro, Ky. 42301. 800-322-8989.

Oak Hill Farms Vidalia Onion Sauce. Sorghum molasses gives this thick-as-mud blend its character. The texture comes from chunks of vidalias, those sweet onions grown only in Middle Georgia. P.O. Box 888302, Atlanta, Ga. 30356. 404-452-8828.

Ollie's World's Best Barbecue Sauce. You can't always tell where you're at by the local sauce. Ollie's, an old Birmingham drive-in, serves a thin, hot, celery seed sauce that'd seem more at home in North Carolina than Alabama. Go figure. 515 University Blvd., Birmingham, Ala. 35205. 205-324-9485.

Rainforest Barbecue. A chunky monkey sort of sauce with ginger, coconut vinegar and other "yummy good stuff from a really far away place" — Sri Lanka. Nature's Key, P.O. Box 1146, New Hyde Park, N.Y. 11040. 800-733-7646.

Razorback. There's Bill Clinton again, on the Razorback brochure with his arm around Red Gill, "Doctor of Porkology." Red's company, River City Spice, bottles a couple of dozen sauces for others. We liked their hot, red house brand. P.O. Box 631, Blytheville, Ark. 72316. 501-763-6392.

Rendezvous. Charlie Vergos' famous cellar specializes in dry ribs smoked with nothing but rubs. But he serves a pretty fair sweet 'n' spicy table sauce, too. 52 S. Second St., Memphis, Tenn. 38103. 800-827-7427.

Rocky Mountain BBQ Sauce. That's not Colorado's Pike's Peak on the label; it's Oregon's Mount Hood. But there's no mistaking the apricot taste inside. TNT Marketing, P.O. Box 1007, Redmond, Ore. 97756. 800-574-2308.

Route 66. This takes the prize for best packaging. It comes in a plastic motor oil container. The sauce? It tastes like it comes in a plastic motor oil container. Still, a must-have for collectors. Famous Foods Inc., P.O. Box 1025, Bristow, Okla. 74010. 918-367-3574

Scott's. One of the best Carolina vinegar sauces. That crimson tint comes from peppers, not tomato — of which this has zip. Shake it up and watch those seasonings swim. P.O. Box 1380, Goldsboro, N.C. 27530. 800-734-SAUC (800-734-7282).

7J Ranch Mesquite. For mesquite lovers only, this tomato sauce comes on like a campfire. Made by D.J. Jardine, who markets a wide variety of Texas sauces. Jardine 7J Ranch, Buda, Texas 78610. 800-544-1880.

Sonny Bryan's. They can't actually bottle Sonny's secret ingredient, brisket drippings.

But they can make a nice shelf-stable approximation of the beefy sauce Dallas loves. 2625 Seelcco St., Dallas, Texas 75235. 800-5-SONNYS (800-576-6697).

Southern Ray's Three Pepper Barbecue Sauce. Like a good fireworks display, this stuff goes off in stages, as jalapeño, red and cherry peppers take turns lighting up the inside of your mouth. Complex, different, very good. P.O. Box 402552, Miami Beach, Fla. 33140. 305-531-0973.

Stubb's Bar-B-Q Sauce. Musicians like Stevie Ray Vaughn used to play for their supper at C.B. Stubblefield's barbecue joint in Lubbock, Texas. He catered for the Rolling Stones, too. We see why. Stubb's peppery, pungent sauce is a regular jumping jack flash. P.O. Box 4941, Austin, Texas 78765. 800-BARBCUE (800-227-2283).

Sumsay Sauces. We could tell these were fusion flavors by the label: a sumo wrestler in a cowboy hat. Brian Koba taps his Japanese-American heritage to make apple-ginger, orange-clove and other cross-cultural flavors. Sur La Table, 410 Terry Ave. North, Seattle, Wash. 98109. 800-243-0852.

Sylvia's. "The Queen of Soul Food," Sylvia Wood, came up with an absolutely unique thin, sweet tomato sauce. Widely available at stores. For information, 212-410-2106.

"21." Yep, the famous Manhattan restaurant has a barbecue sauce, and it's pretty good, even if it does taste more like a steak sauce. Comes in a tall bottle that looks like it could stand next to the Chrysler Building. Available from Dean and DeLuca. 800-221-7714.

Uncle Dave's. The bottle says this is a Southwestern sauce — Southwestern Vermont. It may not be from the barbecue belt, but it's tasty: tart and smoky, with chunks of apple-smoked onions. Cold Hollow Cider Mill catalog, P.O. Box 430, Waterbury Center, Vt. 05677. 800-327-7537.

Upper Mississippi Sauce. This is a sad story about a happy sauce. Jay Rosenthal of Minneapolis took his hot tomato blend to the 1994 American Royal and won first prize. Within a month, he died of a brain tumor. His partners, Pat Kinney and Lissa Michalsky, decided to carry on with Jay's recipe. A fitting last will and testament. P.O. Box 18341, Minneapolis, Minn. 55418. 612-788-4805.

Vernon's Jerk Sauce. Jamaican-born Allan Vernon makes one of the hotter domestic jerks. No salt, no sugar, but lots of spice. 254 W. 29th St., New York, N.Y. 10001. 800-599-JERK (800-599-5375).

Wicker's. They ought to call it Pucker's. The thin, peppery vinegar sauce Peck Wicker started making 50 years ago is all business, the acidic opposite of what they make across state in Kansas City. Widely available in stores in the Mid-South and Midwest. P.O. Box 126, Hornersville, Mo. 63855. 800-847-0032.

Williams-Sonoma Barbecue Sauce. Like a California harvest, this finely balanced blend has a cornucopia of flavors, including raisins, garlic and orange zest. Available April through September. 800-541-2233.

Willingham's W'Ham Sauce. Memphis cook-off champ John Willingham makes a dozen rubs and sauces, including one with chocolate. Willy Wonka at the pit — yum. 6189 Heather Dr., Memphis, Tenn. 38119. 800-737-9426.

Wisconsin Wilderness Berrily Sauce. If you like cranberries as much as tomatoes, this sweet, fruity sauce could be just the ticket. 101 W. Capital Dr., Milwaukee, Wisc. 53212. 800-359-3039.

CATALOGS AND GIFT PACKS

BBQ Buddies. A six-pack of sauces that really looks like a six-pack. Includes Billy Bones, Bourbon Q, Calhoun's of Tennessee, Giovanni's of Chicago, Rasta Joe's of Indiana and Sutphen's of Texas. P.O. Box 3594, Oak Brook, Ill. 60522. 800-222-8348.

Char-Broil. The grillmaker has a terrific "grill-lover's catalog," with dozens of sauces, utensils and, of course, cookers. P.O. Box 1300, Columbus, Ga. 31902. 800-241-8981.

Calido Chili Traders. The fast-growing Kansas-based chain of hot-stuff stores also has a catalog, with more than three dozen barbecue sauces. 800-LOTT HOTT (800-568-8468).

Exclusively Barbecue. This North Carolina mail-order house has everything from grills and barbecue apparel to hard-to-find sauces. Coming soon: a shop in Charlotte. 800-948-1009.

Flamingo Flats. This shop and mail-order business has one of the best sauce selections on the East Coast, with 150 barbecue dressings alone. P.O. Box 441, St. Michaels, Md. 21663. 800-468-8841.

Great Barbecue Sauce Catalog. More than 130 labels from American classics to tasty imports (Aussie Kiwi) to celebrity sauces (Barry Goldwater?). 9538 Hickory Falls Way, Baltimore, Md. 21236. 800-672-8237.

Great Southern Sauce Co. This shop carries a hundred barbecue sauces — and numerous other condiments — and has a catalog. 5705 Kavanaugh Blvd., Little Rock, Ark. 72207. 800-43SAUCE (800-437-2823).

Mo Hotta, Mo Betta. Though they specialize in hot sauces, this mail-order house carries a large selection of spicy barbecue fixin's. P.O. Box 4136, San Luis Obispo, Calif. 93403. 800-462-3220.

Specialty Sauces. This is like buying a whole set of baseball cards. Five famous sauces in one gift pack — McClard's, Sonny Bryan's, Arthur Bryant's, John Wills' of Memphis and Charlie Robinson's of Chicago. P.O. Box 1084, Northbrook, Ill. 60065. 800-SAUCES-1 (800-728-2371).

Weber. The people who make those familiar kettle cookers run an information line from April until Labor Day. Their free pamphlet of cookout basics is well worth having. 800-GRILLOUT (800-474-5568).

Barbecue Societies and Publications

Kansas City Barbecue Society. America's largest barbecue society has members far beyond the banks of the Missouri. Sanctions 50 barbecue cook-offs nationwide and publishes a monthly newspaper, the *Bullsheet*. 11514 Hickman Mills Drive, Kansas City, Mo. 64134. 816-765-5891.

International Barbecue Cookers Association. The largest cook-off circuit in Texas, which has several. P.O. Box 556, Arlington, Texas 76007.

Memphis in May. The other major cook-off circuit, along with the KCBS. They run the world championship in Memphis and sanction 48 other contests. 245 Wagner Place, Suite 220, Memphis, Tenn. 38103. 901-525-4611.

National Barbecue News. Tabloid paper covering the cook-off circuit and other barbecue goings-on. P.O. Box 981, Douglas, Ga. 31533. 800-385-0002.

Still Hungry?

These books are the best we've seen on barbecue:

Asian Grills. Alexandra Greeley. Doubleday, 1993. A cook's tour of the barbecue styles of India, China, Japan and other points East. Asians take this food seriously, maybe more so than we do.

Barbecue Greats Memphis Style. Carolyn Wells. Pig Out, 1989. Fun recipes and stories from that annual Mardi Gras over coals, Memphis in May.
Barbecued Ribs, Smoked Butts and Other Great Feeds. Jeanne Voltz. Alfred A. Knopf, 1990. A lifetime of grilling and good humor by a longtime food editor.

Barbecuing and Sausage-Making Secrets. Charlie and Ruthie Knote. Culinary Institute of Smoke-Cooking, 1993. It may not be slick, but it's one of the most detailed, useful how-to books on the subject. Order from: 2323 Brookwood Drive, Cape Girardeau, Mo. 63702.

Global Grilling. Jay Solomon. The Crossing Press, 1994. This could be the menu if Benetton ever held a cookout for all those cute, multicultural kids in the ads. Chef Solomon offers a rainbow coalition of recipes from around this grilling globe.

Real Barbecue. Greg Johnson and Vince Staten. Harper & Row, 1988. The funniest barbecue road book ever written, with a guide to America's 100 best barbecue joints and thoughts on subjects such as barbecue architecture ("From Bauhaus to Sowhaus").

Texas Barbecue. Paris Permenter and John Bigley. Pig Out, 1994. Texas is a barbecue world unto itself, with distinct traditions and attitudes about sauce. This entertaining survey includes recipes and a guide to the best barbecue joints. Order from: Pig Out Publications, 4245 Walnut St., Kansas City, Mo. 64111.

The Thrill of the Grill. Chris Schlesinger and John Willoughby. William Morrow, 1990. A comprehensive and sophisticated guide drawn from Schlesinger's experience at the East Coast Grill and Jake and Earl's Southern Barbecue in Cambridge, Mass.

Acknowledgments

One of the great things about barbecue is how much people love it. Some people love it so much, in fact, that they'll go to considerable time and effort to help a couple of writers understand how special the barbecue tradition is.

We met dozens of such people in doing this book. We'd like to thank all the cooks, cook-off teams, restaurants and others who shared recipes or gave us advice. We're especially grateful to Thelma Balfour of Memphis in May, Don Gillis and Joe Phelps of the National Barbecue News, Ron Robason of the International Barbecue Cookers Association, and Carolyn Wells and Ardie Davis of the Kansas City Barbecue Society.

We're also appreciative for the help journalistic colleagues gave us: Madeline Drexler in Boston; Christine Arpe Gang in Memphis; John Long and Beth Segal in Cleveland; Doug Cress, Kristin Eddy, Patti Puckett, Eleanor Ringel, Jane Schneider, Sandy Thompson and Jackie Tulloh in Atlanta. We'd particularly like to thank our editors at The Atlanta Journal-Constitution, Lea Donosky and Susan Soper, for their interest and support.

Thanks to John Egerton, who knows as much about Southern foodways as any person alive, for his inspiration. And to Al and Mary Ann Clayton, who not only styled and shot the color photos, but also made many tasty suggestions and helped to keep the project fun. And thanks to John Yow, Chuck Perry and the others at Longstreet Press for putting it all together.

Above all, we'd like to thank our spouses, Pam Auchmutey and Jim Smith, whose editing, recipe-testing, sauce-tasting — and anything else you can think of — made this book possible. They deserve a couple of those tall cook-off trophies.

The cover photo and chapter page photos were shot by Al Clayton, with the exception of the photo on page 2, by Jean Shifrin. The food styling was the work of Mary Ann Clayton.

INDEX

Ah Tong's Special Sauce, 107
Apple City Pork Ribs, 45
Apple City Sauce, 44
Apricot Braai, 96
Arthur Bryant's (restaurant), 7, 20
Asian Barbecued Ribs, 107
Avery Island Barbecue Sauce, 34
Avalon (restaurant), 48

bacon, as major ingredient, 78-79
basil, as major ingredient, 93
Banana Molasses Better-Than-Ketchup, 43
Bangkok Barbecue Marinade And Dipping Sauce, 105
Barney McBee's Texas Goat Sauce, 126
B.B. King's Beale Street Blues Sauce, 24
Beaver Castors, The, 125
beef ribs, how to cook, 82
beer, as major ingredient, 69, 71
Bentley's Good-Enough-For Lafayette Sauce, 31
Bérbere (Ethiopian Peppery Spice Paste), 94
Berry Berry Hot Glaze, 53
Big Bob Gibson's Alabama White Sauce, 117
bison, marinade and sauce, 114
Blackberry-Chambord Barbecue Sauce, 42

black sauce (Kentucky Black Dip), 116
Blount, Roy, 3, 60
blueberry, as major ingredient, 54
bottled sauces doctored, 61
mail-order, 143
bourbon, as major ingredient, 66, 124
Brava Terrace Barbecue Sauce, 69
brine for salmon, 123
brisket, preparation of, 14
Midland Too Brisket Rub, 134

Caffé Barbecue, 72
Cajun Dry Rub, 138
California Barbecued Oysters, 118
Carolina Pig-Pickin' Sauce, 39
Chambord liqueur, as ingredient, 42
Chan Dara (restaurant), 105
Charlie's Zap II Rub, 137
Chef Allen's, 58
cherry, as major ingredient, 50
chicken livers, marinade for, 103
chili, chipotle, as major ingredient, 56, 76
chili, dried, as major ingredient, 88, 90-91
chili, fresh, as major ingredient, 53, 69, 72, 127
chimichuri (Gaucho Green Sauce), 92
Chinois East-West (restaurant), 106

chutney, as major ingredient, 48, 51, 100-101, 127
cilantro, as major ingredient, 57, 105
Coca-Cola Barbecue Sauce, 73
coconut milk, as major ingredient, 102, 105
coffee, as major ingredient, 72, 126
containers, 10
cranberry, as major ingredient, 53
Crescent Dragonwagon's Blueberry Sauce, 54-55
Crescent Dragonwagon's Marinade For Wings, 55
Cuban Mojo Criollo, 89
cumin, as major ingredient, 69, 99, 120-121
Curried Chutney Marinade And Dipping Sauce, 100-101

Daddy Bob's Sit-Down Cider Sauce, 32
Dale's New Orleans Barbecued Shrimp, 119
Dallas Meat-Drippin' Sauce, 27
Danny's Baldheaded Seafood Sauce, 113
Deacon Hubbard's barbecue sauce, 36-37
Deacon Hubbard's Wheat Street Mop, 36
Death Row Bourbon Sauce, 66
Den-Chan's Yakitori Sauce, 109
doctored sauce ideas, 61

Dr. Barbecue's Carolina
  Mustard Sauce, 21
Dragon's Breath, 4
Dreamland (restaurant),
  22-23
Dupree, Nathalie, 71

East Coast Grill (restau-
  rant), 94
Egerton, John, 33
El Paso Chile Company, 76
Ethiopian Peppery Spice
  Paste (Berbere), 94

finishing sauce,
  definition of, 10
For-The-Birds Port-Citrus
  Glaze, 115
Franciscan Zinfandel
  Marinade, 70
Freddie's Hot Honey Sauce,
  25
Fruit-And-Spice Barbecue
  Sauce, 60

garlic, as major ingredient,
  68, 83, 89, 92, 93, 118
Gaucho Green Sauce
  (Chimichuri), 92
George 'n' Ginger Venison
  Marinade, 124
Georgia Peach Marinade
  And Glaze, 46-47
Gilroy Garlic Barbecue
  Dressing, 83
ginger, as major ingredient,
  48, 52, 124
glaze
  Berry Berry Hot Glaze, 53
  For-The-Birds Port-
    Citrus Glaze, 115

Maple-Juniper Marinade
  And Glaze, 80
goat, Barney McBee's sauce
  for, 126
God's Own Dream Sauce, 22
Gore, Al, 132
grapefruit, as major ingredient, 58
Grilled Garlic Wine Sauce,
  68

honey, as major ingredient,
  25, 78-79, 82
horseradish, as major
  ingredient, 74

Indian Dry Rub, 138

Jack Daniel's (see bourbon),
  66
Jamaican
  Dry Rub, 138
  Tim's Jamaican Rum
    rub, 67
Jeanne's Florida
  Horseradish Sauce, 74
jerk
  Upper Mississippi Jerk
    Paste, 86
  Upper Mississippi Jerk
    Pork, 87
Johnny Harris (restaurant),
  30
juniper berry, as major
  ingredient, 80

kebabs
  beef, 100-101
  lamb, 98
  Pork, 47
K.C. Classic, 20

Kentucky Black Dip, 116
King, B.B., 24
Kirk, Paul, 7, 20
Knote, Charlie, 111, 137
Korean Sesame Marinade,
  108
Kosher Cajun Barbecue
  Sauce And Rub, 82
Kreuz Market's We-Don't-
  Need-No-Stinkin'-Sauce
  Rub, 140

lamb
  Marinade for, 103
LBJ's Hail-To-The-Beef
  Sauce, 28
Lemonade Chicken Baste,
  122
lemon grass, as major
  ingredient, 104
Lemon-Thyme Barbecue
  Sauce, 77
Lexington Barbecue
  (restaurant), 29
Lexington Red Splash, 29
Lime-Cilantro Marinade, 57
Louisiana Bacon-Pecan
  Barbecue Sauce, 78-79
low-acid
  Northwestern Low-Acid
    Marinade And Mop, 125
Low-Sodium Orange-Clove
  Sauce, 49

Magic Dust Rub, 45
mango, as major ingredient,
  48
Maple-Juniper Marinade
  and Glaze, 80
marinade
  definition of, 10

safety, 10
Mark Miller's Tamarind
  Chipotle Sauce, 56
Maurice's Piggy Park, 3
Maui Mango-Ginger Sauce,
  48
Meat Doctors Miracle
  Sauce, 26
Mediterranean Dry Rub, 139
Mediterranean Sun-Dried
  Tomato Marinade, 75
Mexican Mole Barbecue
  Sauce And Marinade, 90-
  91
Mexican Dry Rub, 139
Middle Eastern
  Pomegranate-Mint
  Marinade, 98
Midland Too Brisket Rub,
  134
Mongolian Marinade, 106
Moonlite BBQ Drive-in, 116
mop (or sop)
  Deacon Hubbard's Wheat
    Street Mop, 36
  definition of, 9
  Northwestern Low-Acid
    Marinade And Mop, 125
Moroccan-Spiced Yogurt
  Marinade, 97
mustard, as major ingredi-
  ent, 21, 30, 38, 59
My Old Kentucky Sauce, 33

Nathalie's Barbecue Brew, 71
Newman, Paul, 112
New World Grapefruit
  Barbecue Sauce, 58
North-To-Alaska Salmon
  Brine And Rub, 123
Northwestern Low-Acid

Marinade And Mop, 125

Oaxacan Red Chile
  Barbecue Sauce, 88
Obie's Texas Sol Rub, 133
Ol' Hawg's Breath (dry
  rub), 132
orange, as major ingredient,
  49, 115, 120-121
oysters
  California Barbecued
    Oysters, 118

Papa Vito's Ammogghio, 93
Papaya-Ginger Barbecue
  Sauce, 52
parsley, as major ingredient,
  92
Pascal's Manale (restaurant),
  119
Paul Newman's Swordfish
  Marinade, 112
peaches, as major ingredient, 46-47
peanut, as major ingredient,
  64, 102-103
Pear-Mustard Sauce, 59
pecan, as major ingredient,
  78-79
Plum Chutney Barbecue
  Sauce, 51
pomegranate syrup, as
  major ingredient, 98
pork butt
  Upper Mississippi Jerk
    Pork, 87
pork chops
  Maple-Juniper Glazed
    Pork Chops, 81
pork ribs
  Apple City Pork Ribs, 45

Asian Barbecued Ribs, 107
  basic types used, 13
  preparation of, 13
  Sylvia's Oven-Barbecued
    Ribs, 35
pork shoulder
  preparation of, 14
  Upper Mississippi Jerk
    Pork, 87
port, as major ingredient,
  115
Powers, Remus (Ardie
  Davis), 64-65
Prudhomme, Paul, 78

raspberry, as major ingredi-
  ent, 53
Remus' African Groundnut
  Sauce, 64
Rendezvous, Charlie Vergos'
  (restaurant), 129
Rick's Oklahoma-Chicago-
  Mexico Rub, 135
Ron's Real Good Rub, 130
rub
  definition of, 9
  dry, 129-140
  wet
  Tim's Jamaican Rum Rub,
    67
  Vietnamese Lemon Grass
    Wet Rub, 104, 105

salmon, brine and rub for,
  123
Satay Marinade For Beef,
  Lamb Or Chicken Livers,
  103
Satay Marinade For Chicken
  Or Shrimp, 103
Satay Peanut Sauce, 102-103

Savannah-Style Barbecue
Sauce, 30
Scott's South-Meets-South-
Of-France Rub, 131
seafood
Danny's Baldheaded
Seafood Sauce, 113
Secret Asian Sauce, 95
sesame, as major ingredient,
95, 108
shrimp, New Orleans, 119
Satay Marinade For
Chicken Or Shrimp, 103
Tropical Barbecue Sauce
For Shrimp, 120-121
Smoke Signals Sauce, 76
Sonny Bryan's Smokehouse,
9, 27
Spring Creek Bar-B-Que
(restaurant), 4
Stallone, Sylvester, 27
storage, 10
sweet potato, as major
ingredient, 64
sun-dried tomato, as major
ingredient, 75
Swine Lake Ballet Sauce, 38
swordfish, marinade for, 112
Sylvia's Harlem Barbecue
Sauce, 35
Sylvia's Oven-Barbecued
Ribs, 35

table sauce
definition of, 10
tamarind, as major ingredient, 56
thyme, as major ingredient,
77
Tim's Jamaican Rum Rub,
67

Todd's Sweet-Tooth Cherry
Sauce, 50
tofu, marinade for, 127
Tony's Seafood (restaurant),
118
Tropical Barbecue Sauce
For Shrimp, 120-121
Tropical Marinade, 121
Tropical Shrimp, 121
Turkish Marinade With
Cumin And Herbs, 99
Turner Ranch Bison
Marinade And Sauce, 114
Turner, Ted, 114

Upper Mississippi Jerk Paste,
86
Upper Mississippi Jerk Pork,
87

venison, marinade for, 124
Vietnamese Lemon Grass
Wet Rub, 104
Voltz, Jeanne, 74, 85

Wheat Street Baptist
Church, 36
Where's-The-Beef Tofu
Marinade, 127
white sauce (Big Bob
Gibson's), 117
wine, as major ingredient,
49, 68, 70, 118

yakitori
Den-Chan's Yakitori
Sauce, 109
yogurt, as major ingredient,
97
Zarela (restaurant), 88
Zup's Porchetta Rub, 136